County Lines – A Young Person's Guide

By Phil Priestley (2020)

First edition

Contents:

About me & why I'm writing this

Introduction

1. What is county lines?
2. How do you fit into the County Lines model?
3. What are the risks posed to you?
4. How do you get your life back?
5. Who can I turn to for help or advice?
6. How do I help my friend?
7. Looking forward to better things

Postscript

Appendices (resources and support)

About me & why I'm writing this

My name is Phil. I used to be a police officer. A lot of people have different thoughts and feelings when I tell them that. I was police officer, *a copper*, for 17 years. It was a big part of my life. Some people jump to conclusions about what that makes me, and how they feel about me because of it.

Sometimes it's positive and they're really interested – they'd like to be a police officer, or they're curious about what I used to do.

Sometimes it's very negative and they call me a 'pig' or a 'fed' and they treat me with hostility.

In honesty it doesn't matter too much to me either way because I'm used to it now. I mean, it's not nice when people call you a pig or act like you're there to be ridiculed – but that normally happens when that person has an issue that they're struggling with or because of something that happened to them in the past. If they've treated *me* like that, they've probably treated other people like that too – and they might not even know why they do it. *

What I want to reassure you about is that when you read this book you can set that to one side. All that matters about the fact that I used to be a copper is that I know a lot about the subject that we're looking at, and I can give you advice and guidance.

You make your own decisions. Not me. In fact, that's true in school, at home and with your friends – nobody makes your decisions for you. You might feel pushed into certain decisions at times – but if you ever make a decision that you know deep down you didn't really agree with - at the end of the day that decision is always on you.

That's the harsh reality of life.

If you're reading this, you might be anywhere between 11 and 18 years old. There's a massive difference in those seven years.

In years to come you'll have friends who are seven years older than you and seven years younger – but when you're thirty (and believe it or not, that will happen too!) having a mate who is twenty-three, and another friend who is thirty-seven, is just no big deal.

When you're 11 though – the next seven years are just huge.

Some people are 15 years old, they look 21, and they cope emotionally like they are 11.

Some people are 12 years old and they've been caring for close family members since they were

8. Emotionally and mentally they are 16 years old (possibly older). They might look 10.

It's a really complicated time.

There is no standard '15 year old' – not for boys, not for girls or any other identity.

You are you, and as difficult as this is, I'm just trying to write this book *for you*. I won't judge you, I just want to give you information that helps you make the best decisions and choices that you can be happy with.

Why is it a book? Well some people think that books are dead or dying. There's a new multimedia age out there and with Instagram and Tik-Tok and YouTube etc you can probably think of loads of ways you prefer to get information (although you really don't want to see me dancing on Tik-Tok).

The trouble with all those things is that you leave a digital footprint. People see what you download, listen to, view, you have search history (and all that). A good book is a very private thing. Nobody needs to know that you're reading it, where you are with it, or how long it is taking you to get through it. It's just you and your book (if anyone does ask please tell them it's brilliant).

If the power goes out, if the internet drops, if someone else wants the computer — you can always have your book. It's a special thing and I think there is still a place for it.

I also respect young people enough to know that if something is interesting, you'll read it. So I'll try my best for you, and hopefully you'll get a lot out of this and it will be interesting.

But why 'County Lines'? Well — it's a major threat right now. So many young people are getting caught up in this and it has life altering consequences and outcomes.

As a police officer I saw a lot of things. I'm not going to try to shy away from what those things were. This book is real. Very real. Even if you're not easily upset, you might find this a hard read. I'm revisiting things that I don't find easy to think over to be honest.

I got close enough to a number of young people who met with tragic outcomes that really upset me. I'm not going to lie to you — at different times in my career I really struggled with that and I needed to ask for help.

In the 'real world', things do hurt. You don't just brush them off and carry on. When you lose someone, a relationship breaks up, or you or a friend get physically, mentally or emotionally hurt

– it stays with you. You don't just get up the next day and feel fine.

There is enough out there in the world that is negative without having a system of crime targeting you just because of your age and your identity.

County Lines is actually a business model. It creates billions of pounds in revenue for organised crime every year. I'm going to show you how it works, what it is and how come it's happening.

I trust you enough to be mature about that and to have the intelligence and the capacity to deal with it.

In my experience if I treat you like an adult you're likely to respond with that attitude. I respect that. So that's the tone of what I'm writing.

In order for County Lines to make billions of pounds for organised crime it has to victimise young people and children. Reports of young people under 12 are now emerging – but the people behind the County Lines model don't care what happens to these kids. They just want the money.

County Lines is about trafficking drugs. Trafficking means moving drugs from one location to another. Most people think about it as taking something like cocaine from the places where it is made (South America, Columbia is the biggest producer) and getting it out on the streets of the UK.

The part that hurts our young people, if you think about cocaine, is getting that coke into towns and villages easily and for about £10 a go.

Trafficking drugs also includes moving those drugs inside the UK – from London (for example) to Oxford, or Letchworth, or Stoke, or Norwich. If you move a big quantity of drugs – like a kilo of cocaine – from one place to another like that, you are involved in drug trafficking.

The Organised Crime Gangs want to do this because it's very profitable. It's pretty scary how much money they can make on a kilo of cocaine.

Cocaine sells in Columbia for £350 per kilo. On the streets of London, at about £40,000. That's 114 times what that criminal originally paid for it. When they bring the drugs in, they want to bring in tens or hundreds of kilos – as much as they can – because they make more money.

What does come in gets cut down and mixed up with other white powders to make it look like more – and it gets sold like that. So it's not pure cocaine. That way they can make a kilo into two kilos – and £40,000 into £80,000.

The police have tested cocaine that is only 20% pure. That means that someone has turned £40,000 into £200,000. It's all about the money.

Getting young people into carrying, distributing and selling the cocaine is about getting people who are less likely to stand out, who are less expensive to employ, easier to intimidate and bully, and also – you get people who can sell drugs to other children and young people too. Perhaps more scary – *young people are seen as disposable.*

It's not as simple as someone coming up to you and saying "Do you want to sell cocaine for me?" It doesn't happen like that. We do have kids out on the street selling cocaine at 14 years old though. *So how did that happen?*

I want you to know exactly how that happened.

If you turn around one day and you're out there selling cocaine at £10 a bag to people that you don't know, in places you're not familiar with – you've probably got drawn into County Lines. The crazy thing is they know how to get you doing these things in a way that makes you want to do it again and makes you feel good doing it – at least to begin with.

It's a scary place.

If you're in that position right now you probably already regret it and you don't know how to get out.

I want you to know how to get help and how to get your life back.

I know what you are going through and I am sympathetic to you. I want to help you. I'll help you find *a way that suits you* and I won't turn around on you and tell you how disappointed I am (and all that).

Reading this book, you might come from any type of background and you could have dealt with all manner of different things in your life already.

I know from the young people I have already worked with that there is a really strong likelihood that you have been through a lot.

I've met and talked to kids whose dads were murdered, or they walked out on them when they were really little. Whose mum's have been sent to prison or who have got lots of other kids by different guys and that young person doesn't get any time or support at home.

I've talked to kids who have been through sexual and physical abuse, or who live in poverty and they've had enough, or they've had other traumatic experiences. Perhaps they see County Lines as a way out.

Not everyone knows what is driving them or why they do the things that they do.

I understand that.

This book is not just for young people who have got these incredible experiences of hardship or abuse either.

Recent reports say that County Lines' drug dealers are actively seeking what they call 'clean kids'. These are the kids who aren't marked by trauma, haven't been known to school and social services or the police – because these kids just don't get noticed and there is no reason to suspect them.

I've met kids who come from really privileged backgrounds. Public school backgrounds. Wealthy families. They have their own bedrooms in large houses. Mum and Dad both have professional careers. Plenty of money coming in. *Why would someone in that position want to get involved in crime?* We all need something. Believe it or not – every single young person in every single school is worried or concerned about something going on in their lives.

As you get past 12 years old and into your teen years you become a lot more self-conscious. A big part of your brain comes 'online' and switches on. It starts to make you examine yourself, what you did and said, remember things – and it makes you worry about stuff.

We all have insecurity – and even the people who seem more 'with it' and 'together' in everything they do – just struggle in private when they are alone.

I talked to someone for the first time in a long time quite recently – someone I knew from school.

In school I think I was a real mess. I had terrible skin and I got teased a lot for that. I was just very insecure in lots of ways and I didn't know how things around me worked. My self-esteem suffered.

The person that I spoke to recently was one of those people who just seemed really mature – very 'on it' and together – all the way through. She seemed like she was a year beyond everyone else.

She told me she was nearly sick every day before she went to school because she was so anxious. I had no idea.

County Lines' dealers and criminals seek out young people who have these insecurities, but seem mouldable and streetwise. It's not too difficult because everyone has insecurities – but I'm going to show you how they make those things work for them. I'll show you how they turn your insecurities and your self-esteem issues on you, to make you want to do things. We are going to talk about the things that maybe you never thought you'd even think about doing.

It's really powerful stuff actually. If you know what's happening you can stay in control of it. If you don't know how it works, you're vulnerable and it causes you to be weak.

I want you to be strong. The best version of yourself that you can possibly be.

As we go through this book I'm also going to give you some tools that help improve your self-confidence and while some of them might seem odd or make you feel weird - if you're open minded enough, you'll find that some of them work for you.

Nobody has to know that you're reading this, or trying any of the things that I've suggested. If it makes you feel embarrassed – don't worry about that.

We all have an inner voice. It talks to us. Presents us with things. We talk back to it. We talk about the things that we really want to happen. We talk about the things that we really *don't* want to happen. Sometimes it can be quite a nasty voice that tries to persuade us that we're not as good as we really are – but I can help you a bit with that too.

Having a strong inner voice that works for you – and being on the same team as your inner voice – makes you formidable and difficult to beat. It helps you to become someone who can set goals and achieve them – real goals, for your life, that you can be proud of. There is absolutely nothing to be embarrassed about or ashamed of in that.

I'm here to tell you that it doesn't matter what you look like, how you dress, what you own – here and now – if you have control of your own life you can build the person that you want to be.

County Lines is about taking away your control and stopping you from doing that building work. It's about trading your freedom in the long term, for some small gifts, a bit of money and some other things that in a few weeks or months you might not even like or want.

County Lines' dealers like to create drug dependency issues. They want to get people dependent on what they sell – that's obvious – because they'll sell more drugs. This includes having a lot of young people who need to keep coming back for things like cannabis (weed) or other substances (MDMA and Ket both being popular) – but they'll only give you some if you do them 'favours' (or cash).

All of these things take your sense of control away from you. After reading this book I want you to understand that you do have control. That you are an amazing powerful young person who can achieve great things.

I've seen young people from situations where they are really disadvantaged, go and achieve amazing things – it takes hard work and determination. If you are focused enough you can become the person that you want to be.

I don't think the person that you want to be is drug dependent or under the control of an organised criminal gang – but if you feel drawn to that we can look at why you might feel that way. County Lines is designed to be as attractive as possible – and they're pretty good at making something really dark and bleak look cool and worthwhile.

So I don't start with any presumptions about you. I don't pretend to know you intimately – but I hope that my words reach you off this page in the way that I intend. That is, that you can tell how much I care.

You might be a person who is surrounded by people who tell you they love you and show you that they love you. You could be someone who feels hugely let down by the adults in your life.

What I want you to understand is that I'm grateful that you opened this book, and that in reading my words, you're allowing me to be a voice in your life. That's a powerful privilege and I don't take it for granted. You might not agree with everything that I say in every chapter – *don't let that put you off*. I don't agree with everything that I used to believe in – and confusingly – as I get older I change and I evolve as a person. I'm able to listen to people who I don't agree with just to be able to understand what they do believe in and try to understand why. If there is something in this book that you feel is so argumentative and wrong that you want to put the book down, I ask you to carry on – keep reading – and when you're done, look at the things you do agree with, and the things that you don't agree with, and weigh them up.

At the very least we will have a conversation and you're making informed choices. This is not a bedtime story – *and we are about to get into it!*

You might decide that this book is a starting point for you and you want to read other things that I and other people have written – *that would be really good*. As you open your mind and broaden your understanding you begin to realise that freedom is found in your ability to use critical thought and to think for yourself.

All of these aspects are closed down for you when you get into a County Lines operation. Gangs are run on defining behaviour codes, acceptable fashions, telling people what to do – and having to be the person that they want you to be.

This book is about lighting up the individualism you have. If you're involved in County Lines right now, it's about giving you that ability to do that again.

You are *not* trapped. You don't have to do what any of these people say you have to do. It doesn't matter how intimidating or threatening they are.

I'm also going to show you how you reach out to a friend that you're worried about – how you get expert advice and guidance and how you help them. I'm going to show you what I think good friendship is and what the best of friends do for each other in these circumstances.

It takes real courage to be a good friend when you see someone that you care about and have known for a long time, getting involved in something like this.

First of all – just by reading this book you'll be able to spot the signs and symptoms before most other people (including adults and professionals).

Secondly – what you then choose to do will take a lot of guts and it might not feel like the thing that you would expect. Being a friend who just says 'yes' and goes along while their friend makes mistakes and gets themselves hurt – that's no type of friend at all. Particularly if you can see what is coming down the line.

We'll look into that – and how you can be the best type of friend – and if that friend really lets you down and ends up exposing you to risk and harm, when do you cut that friend off?

It's an awful conversation – but let's be honest – the thought goes through your mind.

The advice that I'm going to give you *is for you*. Not your mum or dad, or your teacher. I'm writing this for you.

In this format (a book) you know that the advice I am giving is consistent. That is, it's the same advice I give to the next person who reads this book. Why is that important? Well you need to be aware that some people will say whatever suits them from one moment to the next. Such people advise others to do things because it's what's good for themselves (and not the person they are advising). When someone has the courage to write a book, they really make it clear where they stand, and they have to stand there. If you write a book and later change your position, you change it for everyone – *and you have to explain why*.

The advice and guidance that is here in this book for you is the same advice and guidance that I would give to the son or daughter of a millionaire, or a billionaire, a member of royalty, a senior politician... you know you're getting the best advice I can give you. This advice isn't written for any of those people though – the person I want to reach *is you*.

You'll be used to people doing things to encourage social media follows, likes, subscriptions, donations, and crowdfunding. There is none of that here. Nothing that I am writing in this book depends on the idea that I want you to become a follower or a subscriber or something like that.

In a lot of ways I'm quite stubborn and independent. If thousands of people want to go the other way, I personally won't follow the crowd. I don't expect the crowd to follow me and I'm not here to try to get them to do that.

When you feel confident enough, and comfortable enough to be in that position, you know that you can't be pushed into doing something that will harm you. If I make a mistake it is on me and I take responsibility for it – but I won't look across at someone else and say "He made me do it".

Likewise, I'm not going to stop halfway through the book and give you some words from a sponsor. I won't tell you that a brand of trainers are great or that you should drink a refreshing can of whatever. We're not going to be interrupted in the middle of a paragraph by a downloadable app that will change your life, download it for free and all that rubbish.

There's a time and place for all that – but that's not here. This is a time and a place that is just about you and nobody else. It's about encouraging independent critical thinking – your own ability to make up your own mind about what you like and don't like, what you trust and don't trust and most importantly, who you want to be in your life time.

One of my favourite quotes, from a hero of mine (and we all have different heroes) is from a guitarist called Jimi Hendrix. He was an amazing musical genius. Tragically he died at the age of 27 following a drugs overdose. He had a unique sense of style and art that drew a lot of attention and criticism but also reshaped so much of what we now know. He said:

"I'm the one that's got to die when it's my time to die, so let me live the way I want to."

I want to help you to live the way that you want to – and with regard to this subject, County Lines, I want you to make a choice that is based on the facts and true knowledge of what it's all about. Then you can live the way that you want to live.

Thank you for reading my book.

Phil

Introduction

Ok, so I kind of *have* introduced the subject and put it on the table for you.

There are two main issues within this book that are equally important:

What County Lines is, and

Who you are?

Let's keep it simple. Outside of those two questions there is nothing else in the whole world.

The fact is that, if you can sort out the second question — which is the biggest and the most important question of all — you don't need to worry about County Lines. You'll be bigger than pretty much anything else out there too.

Some people seem to walk into the world with a sense of purpose and commitment — they just seem to stride out there. There's no sense of timing — they could appear at any time in history and the whole of history would wrap around them. You know it for a fact.

I look at Bill Gates and Steve Jobs as two examples of this — they saw circuit boards and microprocessors and then knew how to change the whole world with them.

Bill Gates is the man that most people know as being behind Microsoft. When he started out people laughed at him because he said that there was going to be a computer on every desk. *The fact was at that time there were maybe twenty computers of one sort or another in the world – and the big computers took up whole rooms.*

Bill Gates was convinced that was rubbish. He was told that there would never be more than a hundred computers in the world. He just knew that was untrue. *Now we've got people buying fridges with computers in them that talk to you.*

If Bill Gates had been born in the 1800s he'd have been developing trains or steam power, or manufacturing new versions of steel. He doesn't operate down there in the 'can't do' bracket. So we, sort of, see him as something more than human.

Growing up Gates was the absolute nerd – I mean if you look at the photos of him – this is not a kid concerned about fashion, looks and all those types of things. His dad was a lawyer, he had a comfortable background and some advantages with that – and yes he was gifted with a really impressive brain and an ability to think clearly –

but none of that means he's going to grow up and make $100 billion (literally what he did).

When people talk to Gates now the money is not even the achievement as far as he's concerned – he's a man who changed the world and influenced the whole of humanity. That's a pretty heavyweight achievement. *There are richer people* – well at least one richer person – the rest is a debate about what any of these types of people are really stashing away – but everyone agrees that the guy who owns Amazon is richer. I don't think Jeff Bezos would argue that his online shop is more significant to humanity than creating Microsoft though.

My point is that such people work on their self-knowledge – *and it's true of many other people who don't end up sat on $100 billion, but still do amazing things anyway*. They get in touch with what is important to them, what they value and they really understand who they are.

If you can answer that question ("Who are you?") beyond just giving your name – you become a rock – you become a monument. There are millions (billions) of adults walking around right now who *can't* answer that question. Every day they get up and go to work just to pay the bills, put food on the table, watch a bit of TV and do the same tomorrow.

If by the end of this book you can come one step closer to an understanding of yourself – and an understanding of your personal history and where you have come from – believe me, you have made achievements right there that will intimidate others and throw you towards your dreams and ambitions.

People who don't know themselves get swept along with whatever other people are doing. People get hysterical and move in packs. You've seen it, and I've seen it. You've done it and I've done it. Collective excitement and being in the peer group is just one of those things that appeals to human beings in a very bold way.

If you look at animals in the wild *they tend to move in packs*. They stay safe in numbers and they move together. If they stay together there is less chance they'll get eaten by a predator. Their whole existence is about staying on their feet, staying in the pack, eating, drinking and repeating that without getting eaten by something. Our defensive instinct is to just stay inside that pack and mimic the person next to you.

This only really works if your pack is trustworthy and you are mimicking the behaviours of someone who is reliable and who is doing the right things. If you are following and mimicking the wrong people the outcomes can be very negative.

Some people are more ambitious and you might compare them to the natural predators or pack leaders. The are naturally more confident, aggressive, and assertive. They don't mind standing out from their group.

It really is your choice as to how you feel and who you believe you are. Ultimately though – it is a lack of self-knowledge that tends to put you in difficult or dangerous positions.

I want you to read this thinking – *"if I don't want to be the predator, or the herd leader, I need to know how to find and recognise a herd that is right for me. One that I can really be safe in"*.

I don't want you being a gazelle hanging with a pack of hyenas thinking you're safe. Believe me – County Lines is very much about persuading you that you fit somewhere and to be something that 99% of the time is not right for you (Organised Crime Gangs don't care about such things).

If you look into yourself and find you've got ambition to be something more aggressive and assertive (within your community) – that's great – but I want you to choose to do that in a way that is good for you, is genuine, and actually makes the best use of that drive. People who don't have the same drive will happily recognise that in you and get you to go out and achieve things for them (but they'll expect you to bring it back and lay it at their feet for them). This is when you're getting 'used'.

Either way — *we have to gain self-knowledge* — sometimes challenge our instincts — and make the best decisions that we can. **That's a big part of this book. Without even getting into the questions around 'County Lines'.**

Being perfectly honest, getting trapped into a situation through County Lines is not the real problem — it's the symptom of the broader problem which is a lack of self- awareness. *We have to be wise enough to see through that and see past it.*

I want you to establish a better sense of who you are — and you'll then be able to look at County Lines and say whether that works with what you want from your life. I doubt that it will.

I'm not going to lie — I hope you reach the conclusion that County Lines makes no sense once you get to that point. Most of the people that make the mistake of getting involved in County Lines only *then* realise who they really are and find out what they want (by going through something really hurtful).

Very often, that's just too late. It's tragic when that happens. If you've been harmed by County Lines, and then you realise that what you wanted in life was way over there – somewhere else – you probably feel like you already ruined your chances. When I see that happening, *it's heart breaking.*

You might be involved in County Lines already – but you're thinking that you want something very, very different. *So let's talk about how we get you out of there and to that other place where you really want to be instead.*

Life might be about the money for you – you might want to be a millionaire, billionaire, and all of that. There is nothing wrong with wanting to achieve financial success. A lot of success is put forward in terms of how much money a person has made.

It's really not the only measure of success. There's also a very strong argument that with self-knowledge and the ability to become the very best at anything, you can and will achieve a very healthy level of financial prosperity and independence (without making the money define who you are and who you want to be).

There are plenty of people who think that just making money will satisfy them – but no matter how much they make, or what they buy with it — it's just pointless and they feel empty or perhaps they just need to make more? They thought their first million would feel wonderful. *Maybe they need a hundred million?*

In truth, they've only just found out (or they're starting to learn) that it's not money or the things that money can buy that makes them feel successful. With better self-knowledge they could have been happier people.

If you do want to make yourself financially rich — *and you can*, and if you are determined to do it, *you will* — I want you to be happy and proud of yourself while you are doing it and when you achieve it. There are plenty of people who are very happy to be wealthy, and they've got it absolutely right for themselves. That might be you — but the chances are that selling drugs to get there is not realistic.

So while we talk about County Lines, forgive me if I keep coming back to this issue about self-knowledge and who you want to be. I think that's the most important question of all. I genuinely think if you get up a level on that — you'll not have any worries about County Lines, apart from maybe being a strong enough person to help protect your friends.

Thinking back to the images that we had of the herd animals in the wild – let me tell you certainly – County Lines as a system is a method of getting predators into the herd of prey. The system is designed to make you feel like while it's happening you're a predator – when actually you're a gazelle being led away to meet the rest of the hungry lions.

There are plenty of enemies to confront in the world – but probably the most difficult and hurtful are false friends.

There are some people who work their way into your life, and you end up developing feelings and loyalties for them. When such people turn on you it hurts you more than anything else. You find it hard to believe, but they're absolutely ready to hurt you when the time comes.

From time to time we all confront people and issues – *head-on* – that we know we are opposed to. There is something honest and respectable about that. In that situation we can disagree – but respect the fact that the person we disagree with is up front about their position. We use that term "Agree to disagree".

People who lie and position themselves outside of your radar, who give themselves the ability to attack you from behind, who get into your personal information, or inside your head or your heart – that's something that nobody can respect or agree with. It's deeply harmful on a different level.

Getting into the business end of what we're doing here – we're talking about a form of self-defence – and as much as possible I want you to be really good at avoiding those situations.

The easiest form of self-defence belongs to people who can see the confrontation from a mile away – and decide not to put themselves into it in the first place.

"I can see you coming, with your drama and your grief, but I'm too wise for that. I'm crossing the street."

You don't take people on face value – *you make an assessment of what they are all about, what their motives are, and what's going on really. You proceed with caution – you watch them carefully – you see who they are in their actions, not in their words.*

If you get good at that, the friendships that you choose to make afterwards will be strong and reliable ones, and the likelihood of being let down is much smaller.

In life we will always have to cope with the unexpected, with heart break, with adversity and what we would describe as 'bad luck'. These things will happen – nobody is so wise and so nimble that they can just avoid this stuff 100%. In life 'shit happens'. True?

The truth is that certain aspects of life – including the painful times are inevitable. If you have a good plan, and good self-awareness, you will ride those times out and get back to feeling happier and more satisfied. You'll go back to the good times.

People who don't have a plan or a direction tend to bounce from drama to drama – they even get hooked on the emotional charge that they get from being in a drama. It gives them a sense of purpose. They look for dramas that other people are tied up in – they make their whole focus in life upon that. You never see them genuinely achieve anything from it though. These people are always loud, always have a lot to say, always wade in – but inside themselves there is a sense of emptiness, and it's very sad.

For people who seek out drama – who lack self-knowledge – and bounce from mistake to mistake – County Lines is made to scoop them up. Without any doubt whatsoever. People running County Lines can see these people from a distance. They are vulnerable in a way that can't be described properly. They have chaotic lives, there's no order or structure, they're not building towards anything, and their aspirations are very limited.

They never sat down to ask themselves — honestly — who am I? What am I good at? What have I practised? What do people know me for? What do I want?

An additional — and really important strand of self-knowledge is about being able to see our limitations and our weaknesses. We need to learn to apologise to others if we make mistakes and let them down. We need to realise that there is no expectation of being perfect. We need to become friends to ourselves before we can trust other people to feel the same way about us.

Developing this form of self-awareness leads us towards sympathy, empathy and compassion.

Some people start on a level that called 'pity' — pity is seen as a deeply negative thing. It's quite a shallow emotion that is a long way from connecting the person experiencing it from what they are seeing. It basically acknowledges that other people exist.

Empathy is a funny word. It's a lot like sympathy and sometimes people use one word instead of the other. They're actually quite different.

Being sympathetic is about seeing someone who is struggling, having a hard time, experiencing a form of pain — and being able to literally feel those feelings too from your own perspective. You understand what they're going through – you might feel profoundly bad as a result. The bottom line is that you care.

Empathy is an acknowledgement that is further on from this. It includes the ability to anticipate how another person would feel in a set of circumstances. You can anticipate things from perspectives that aren't just focused on you. More than this you can actually apply a more constructive approach to it and maybe begin to help that person out.

Sympathy and empathy evolve to become compassion. Compassion is what we demonstrate when we start to do something positive that helps someone else and the world around us. You actually start to get involved.

Let's consider a homeless person, sleeping in a shop doorway.

Some people can walk by and act as if that person isn't even really there. They don't get hurt or upset by seeing it because they almost tell themselves it's just not real and (of course) it could never happen to them.

Pity happens when the person walking by does recognise that there is a person there – but they can't relate to it on any level, they don't feel to blame – they might make it easier to deal with by telling themselves something like "We all have the same chances in life – they just didn't work hard enough" (or something like that). They do feel bad – but it's a judgmental thing, and it's not helpful.

Sympathy happens when the homeless person is acknowledged by the person walking by – and they see them, feel bad *for* them, and allow themselves to wish that person had a better situation. They don't venture towards helping or doing anything constructive about it though.

Empathy takes us forward again – now the person sees the homeless person in the doorway – they might even be able to put themselves in that situation for a fleeting moment. *"It must be horrible to have to stay there tonight, and it's going to be very cold…"* They might consider the possibility that the person has tried their best, and might not be to blame for the situation they're in. This is how we tend to treat ourselves.

So instead of feeling for that person, they are now feeling *with* that person. They empathise.

Eventually we arrive at compassion. The person is moved by the sight of a homeless person, they regret that society doesn't do enough for the homeless, they blame themselves for not doing more, and they begin to reach out and try to do something. This might be something as small as buying a sandwich and a hot drink. *They've now demonstrated compassion.*

A lack of compassion, empathy or sympathy is broadly an outstanding way to show people that you don't understand yourself and that your spectrum of self-awareness is pretty shallow.

As we begin to learn about ourselves it actually becomes more difficult to hurt other people. We are more likely to be forgiving of the people around us, as we realise that there have been lots of times that we have needed other people to forgive us.

Seeing our own imperfections, we tend to be more tolerant and accepting of other people and their imperfections. People who go from a position of having very low levels of self-awareness, who then begin to realise that – and start to achieve self-awareness – they sometimes feel really embarrassed and ashamed of how they used to be. So if you do achieve that – either reading this book or any other material – you have to be ready for that discomfort. It's not an easy process.

Within this book we're on a journey. We want to make you emotionally more intelligent, more compassionate and more aware of the world around you. We want you to be able to see trouble before it approaches you, so that you can stay well out of the way.

We want you to know what matters to you – and what you want out of your life. I want to reassure you that no matter what your dream, goal or ambition is – you can get there. I don't just believe in that – it's as certain to me as night follows day.

I want you to finish this book and be able to have a plan for yourself – written down or not written down. The fact is, the people who have plans for themselves are not the people who get sidetracked by exploitative people, crime, drugs and getting into trouble. They're too focused on getting what they want.

If you can get there you'll be a stronger person, a better friend to the people around you, and without a shadow of a doubt you'll be prouder of yourself every day of your life. There's also a much stronger likelihood that when you do achieve your goals and dreams, they'll satisfy you – because you'd really understood what those achievements were going to be all about before you even made them.

This couldn't be further from a 'just say no!' (to drugs) message. In fact, it's a 'just say yes!' (to life) message instead. I want you to imagine your goals and your dreams and I want you to be totally taken up by saying 'yes' to them.

If you understand your goals and dreams – you'll immediately understand for yourself (and you won't need me to explain it to you) how County Lines threatens those precious things that are so important to you.

If we can get there together – you'll absolutely appreciate the rest of the advice in this book, which is all about how you avoid County Lines and the trauma that it brings into your world. You'll take one look at it for yourself and you'll see it for exactly what it is.

I don't want you to feel that any advice I offer to you is intended to deny you something, or to prevent you from having something – I want you to see this advice is about fighting for your goals and dreams. It's about giving you the resilience to never give up on the things that really matter to you in life. It's about respecting you and caring enough about you to let you make the positive choices.

One of the things I got told commonly by addicts and people with lives ruined by drug dependency and crime is that nobody ever took them to one side and really told them when it could've made a difference. *Nobody stopped them*. They talk about fantasy situations "I wish I could go back in time and talk to myself".

If it helps you – imagine that *you* wrote this book. You wrote this book to yourself in twenty years time, and sent it back through time to tell yourself something that you really needed to know right now. *"Hey – pay attention to this – if you get this right we're gonna become a _____"* (put your dream in there).

So as we go through this book – remember that it was written very particularly for you. It comes from someone who cares about you and believes in you. It is focused on helping you to be a stronger and more successful person. It comes from someone who wants you to achieve all of your goals and dreams and ambitions. It also happens to have a lot of content that relates to an active threat posed to young people in our communities right now – and if you're not switched on to this threat – it could really damage your dreams and goals in the worst way.

So that's your introduction really.

Unlike a story or a fiction this book doesn't have to be read in a particular order (although it is in a particular order, to be fair). You can come back to this introduction at any time if you need to remind yourself of it or any of the stuff that is within it. The same is true of any of the chapters. There might be one chapter – or part of one chapter – that means a lot more to you and really stands out. This 'thing' just happens to address something very personal to you. Come back to it when you need to.

You can do that. It's your book, it's your journey and it's your personal space and time. Nobody gets to tell you how it goes. The only test is life.

Chapter One: What is County Lines?

Let's start talking about what County Lines is. Basically every business — and by business I'm talking about any operation that is motivated by making profit and generating money — has a plan. It is organised in a certain way and it is run with a particular structure.

You can think about any of the most successful brands that you really like and they work exactly the same way. Apple, Samsung, Louis Vuitton, Disney — no matter how creative and how strong their presentation is — they look like pure fun on the outside, but inside they are all business.

You don't get to the top without being absolutely on point with your planning and you stick to that planning with a type of determination that defies everything else.

Even when you're not in business, if you want to get from one place to another — you need a plan.

Athletes that win Olympic medals have plans.

When you go from your house to the shops you have a plan.

If you don't follow the plan you don't get to your destination.

County Lines is nothing more than a plan. It's the latest successful plan for distributing illegal drugs and making as much money as possible doing it. It has completely taken over the way that illegal drugs are sold in the UK – and I'm going to tell you exactly how and why.

First of all it started in the main cities. In the cities – like London (being the biggest of our cities) the competition for selling and buying drugs has become lethal. We got to a point in April 2018 where murder rates in London were higher than New York (and not because the New York murder rate was falling – it wasn't).

Now organised criminal gangs don't really care about that unless they are feeling that threat very personally – foot soldiers and innocents are not that much of a concern – but what does worry them is profitability and people getting paid.

When competition is high people try to get new customers – so if you were running a gang you'd have lots of people trying to sell to *your* customers.

To do this they'll do lots of things – like offering credit, or selling drugs cheaper, or selling with more purity in their drugs (remember when we talked about people breaking cocaine down to 20% purity? If your purity has to be 50% that is a lot less profit for you – your cost of business is more than twice as high).

Fighting over small areas became known as 'postcode wars' and gangs fought (and fight) over territories in which they could be the main or the only supplier of drugs.

Remember – if you're the only supplier in an area your prices can go up, the quality of your product can go down, and people are still going to queue up and buy from you.

All the time while this was happening other parts of the country were broadly undisturbed by what was going on. Villages and towns across the UK had lots of potential drug buyers' in them – but the gangs were fixated over fighting for their postcodes in London, Birmingham, Liverpool, Manchester and so on.

The first thing about County Lines is that it reaches outside of those postcodes and reaches into the villages and towns across the UK – and treats them like an export market.

If you invent something really amazing – like a new revolutionary way to vacuum – you're eventually going to sell as many vacuum cleaners as you can in the UK. You're going to have to find a way to sell them in America, in Australia, in the

Far East and Africa – all over the world. This is the export market.

So County Lines treats everywhere outside of the major city like that – an export market.

To do this they need someone who runs packages of drugs out to those areas.

Then they need a method of offering those drugs to as many people as possible.

Then they need to supply them and take the cash

Finally the cash has to come back into the gang leader.

The whole situation can then repeat.

The County Line is actually a telephone number. A simple mobile phone number. It's a burner phone that isn't registered to anyone and that can be ditched in a minute if the police pick it up or 'compromise' it.

The buyer phones the number or sends a message (usually an sms message) and says what they want.

The person on the other end of the line gets in touch with that person they have locally and tells them to deliver – weed, cocaine, heroin, MDMA, whatever it is – and they get the money there and then (a bit like 'JustEat').

So this involves a person who carries a large amount of drugs (remember – trafficking) out of, say, London, to somewhere like Huntingdon in Cambridgeshire (a small town) or Sawston (a village). They sit on that and they hide it from the authorities – the police mainly – and try to keep their head down from people who might prosecute them or take action against them.

This person – this sitter - will do two things mainly – they'll recruit other people to do the running around, delivering drugs and collecting cash. They'll also try and get that mobile number into the hands of as many drug users as they possibly can.

This means handing it round at parties. Waiting in places where users hang out (like outside pharmacies first thing in the morning, waiting for methadone prescriptions). What they really want to do is get young people to sell to other young people because that's the new drug market growing up.

Heroin is a very profitable drug because it encourages addiction and it is bought from a very poor part of the world. People who use heroin smoke it or inject it – injecting it (intravenous drug use) is particularly addictive because it goes straight into the blood stream and from there it hits your brain in seconds.

Heroin users who go 'on the needle' are doomed. They're absolutely certain to become addicted.

The first hit of heroin that a person ever takes is always the best they are ever going to have. They are completely 'clean' – so just a small amount of heroin will have an effect on them that will never ever be replicated in future. Over time the hits won't ever be quite as intense or enjoyable – and every next hit will be ever so slightly less satisfying (demanding that users consume more).

Most heroin users go from being concerned about the high, or to trying to get the same level of high, to eventually just trying not to go into a painful state of detox. They eventually just take heroin to try to feel normal and behave like everyone else walking around in public – without heroin they start getting physically ill.

Heroin is a dirty drug and like cocaine it gets cut up with all kinds of rubbish to make the shipment last longer. It is an import drug that is brought in from the poppy fields of Afghanistan.

Heroin is also a terrible drug for life consequences. Users who move into needle abuse do significant damage to their veins and it's not uncommon to see people who have abused for many years who have lost limbs as a result. They've literally had a foot or their lower leg removed because of the damage caused, and they suffer weeping sores and infections that won't heal.

When something is as addictive as heroin it gets very expensive and commonly heroin addicts will turn to stealing things to pay for their hit. So they might break into cars, they might burgle houses, they might steal from shops. They'll steal something worth a lot of money (like a TV, or a fancy mountain bike) and they'll sell it for next to nothing because they are desperate to get money together to buy a little bit more heroin — they'll take whatever they can get.

When they use they 'nod out' — which means that they go into a sleep like state. They're somewhere between asleep and sedated. They are totally unaware of where they are and they don't care about their appearance or who can see them like that.

Homelessness is a big consequence of heroin addiction because most hardened heroin addicts would rather buy 'gear' than pay rent and have a roof over their heads. Heroin abuse keeps people on the streets and unable to recover their footing financially.

Over-use (overdose) on heroin is fatal and kills people. Commonly if someone goes to prison as a consequence of what they were doing to support their addiction, they might come out looking for heroin and take a hit that is like something they'd been able to tolerate before they went inside. Their body no longer has that tolerance and they overdose accidentally. Alternatively they just buy from a different dealer who has a different purity level – and a simple purity change in the market could be enough to result in an overdose.

So the fact is that a lot of people are wary about heroin. For good reasons. When I first started policing there was an epidemic of heroin abuse – it was just everywhere. Teenagers were getting into it, and people in their twenties and thirties had already been hooked for years. To be fair not many users get much beyond their forties.

It was a really horrible time.

Stats tend to show that heroin is a less popular drug now and although it's still profitable and highly addictive – it's not what drug dealers will be depending on to sell in the future (unless people change their minds).

I'm really happy that young people aren't getting into heroin at the rate they once were. I hope that the whole heroin culture dies away (it probably won't but I hope it does).

What this means for County Lines is that either they encourage a load of young people to get back into heroin or they get young people buying other things instead.

To do this they need to have access to young people to begin with.

This is part of the reason why County Lines wants to attract young people in — recruitment — and to get them selling. If they can get young people selling in schools and colleges the illegal drug business will grow and become more profitable.

When or if the heroin generation dies away it will be replaced by either new heroin users or people using other drugs — but overall the market for drugs is surprisingly stable.

The other main drug that is very profitable is cocaine — coke — *also sold as crack.*

Crack is a form of cocaine that hits harder and is more addictive. Unlike heroin — which is steadily in decline — coke and crack are still hugely popular and there is no end in sight.

Both drugs — coke and heroin are clearly the most dangerous and threatening drugs out there. You ought to know that if you get into heroin or coke you're going to get an addiction and it will ruin you financially (in 99.9% of cases).

Young people tend to be wary of heroin, coke and crack, so County Lines is about offering other drugs too. The third (very) popular drug is cannabis or weed. Weed has a really strong reputation with children and young people as being a soft drug, that's not dangerous and as such it's easier to sell to young people than crack or heroin.

A lot of people now have false ideas about weed - that it is really very good for you – that it cures diseases and does positive things for your body.

While it *has* been used in medical trials for different purposes, nobody is promising the kind of things that you hear about on social media, even in the countries where it is legal to buy and sell weed.

Cannabis doesn't cure cancer (sadly). It has been used as a method of reducing pain and discomfort in chronic illnesses that I hope you never get – but if you don't have those illnesses (like M.S. or terminal cancer) it's like reaching for a paracetamol when you don't have a headache.

Getting high won't kill you – there's no evidence of fatalities connected to using cannabis – and that's why it's a class B drug, not a class A drug like heroin or crack — but that doesn't mean it doesn't cause harm.

A lot of people use it and start to rely on it to help them when they are struggling with poor mood, anxiety, or stress. The truth is that you learn how to cope with these things the older you get. Your brain hasn't finished developing and doesn't really finish until you hit about 21 years old. Using cannabis can mean that the developmental stages you go through in your teenage years don't happen properly, and you struggle to manage your emotions, your anger, your highs and your lows for the rest of your life.

There is no evidence that weed causes psychosis (the most serious forms of mental illness) but what experts do believe is that if you are 'susceptible' (for example there's a risk that you could develop a form of psychosis due to family history) cannabis makes it more likely that it will happen to you.

County Lines needs kids smoking lots of weed — it's very profitable, it's not a drug that has to be imported because it can be produced in false environments in the UK. It also gets another generation into drugs generally — and the more people smoking weed, the more chance there is that you could also sell MDMA or get them to try something else synthetic like Spice.

There's one thing that you really need to know about weed though – street 'purities' (that is the strength of cannabis out on the street) is just rising all the time.

Even when compared to ten years ago – cannabis now is much stronger than it was. This is because of what cannabis is made up of.

Cannabis has two main parts – THC and CBD. THC is a substance that basically tickles your brain in different way and gives you a ride when you take it. In small amounts this is funny, and makes you feel good and might make you laugh and smile. It's like being in a fast car and enjoying it a bit when it goes a bit faster and you have to hold on tight. You get a similar sense of being out of control – but being entertained and animated by it.

CBD is like a cushion – it's the thing that acts like the airbag and the seatbelt. It protects your brain and softens the slow-down* of the ride. It's the more chilled out part of the drug that makes you feel sleepy or just calmer.

Weed has a reputation for being a calm chilled out experience – but street weed has far more THC in it now, and a lot less CBD – so the actual experience can be quite scary. People get panic attacks, anxiety, and they can feel very alarmed by it. It's not what they thought it was going to be.

After using it you can feel very hungry and you can also feel very grumpy and angry for no reason. Anger management problems are common and we're seeing a lot more young people struggle with anger because of weed.

You're probably not going to smoke weed and develop a psychosis overnight. You're not going to drop down dead. For most people their first experience of smoking weed is either something they enjoy a lot, or something they just didn't like. A few people have an immediate high that is very consuming, a similar number have a really awful experience.

One way or the other weed is part of a triangle of drugs that are being supplied through County Lines – heroin, coke and weed. In addition there are lots of other drugs – MDMA (ecstasy), LSD (which is making a big come back), ketamine (or 'ket'), spice (which is a form of cannabis made in a laboratory but with a huge amount of THC) – and depending on the setting a County Lines dealer will try to be available with whatever a local community is demanding and is ready to pay money for.

Of course all of this is highly illegal and there are serious prison sentences for people who possess drugs with intent to supply them or get caught supplying.

The police have enforcement tactics that include stop and search (to find people in possession of drugs) and test purchasing (which is where an undercover officer buys drugs from a supplier through the County Line). People can and do go to prison for these offences.

The reason that dealers are willing to risk going to prison is because the drugs market makes so much money. Recent estimates of the illegal cannabis market was over £2 billion across the UK. Nobody is paying any tax on those profits either.

It's a live fast and die young type of experience – the more successful you become selling drugs, the harder it is to hide that money from the authorities. Once the authorities notice that you've suddenly got a lot of money people start asking where that money came from. A teenager can't just walk into the bank with regular amounts of money – a thousand pounds cash here and a thousand pounds cash there – so where are you going to hide it?

It can get to the point where you can't physically spend the money either — if you're walking around in Louis Vuitton tracksuits and the newest limited edition Nike Trainers — people are going to ask where they came from too.

The New York rapper Jay-Z is open about the fact that, at one time, he was selling crack cocaine in the poorest areas of New York. A very dangerous business – but again very profitable. He wrote the line

"Keep coke in coffee

Keep the smell of money off me"

Talking about how he was always thinking about how to hide drugs and cash — the smell of drugs (drugs dogs) and the consequences — 'the smell of money'. So even if you don't walk around with money in your hands, even if you're not putting it over the counter at the bank, if you're walking around in a Louis Vuitton Supreme hoodie — you literally smell like money.

County Lines is all about driving those profits higher. Get children and young people selling drugs — get that money back into the city to the main guy, the 'top boy' and he tries to 'launder' it so that it appears that it has been earned legally (at least by him).

The dealers on the street get some rewards to keep them doing it – but they run all the risks of being arrested and prosecuted, beaten up or even killed by other dealers.

The levels of violence that grew up in the cities has followed the County Lines model out of those areas and into the rest of the UK. The same 'rules' and expectations apply.

So carrying knives and weapons is really common. It's not just about carrying a knife either (which is a criminal offence) it's about being ready to show people that you're going to use it. There's only one way to do that – stab someone.

We talked about how violence in the cities had got out of hand.

As I write this we've had news reports this weekend about several stabbings in a major incident in Birmingham (6th September 2020).

Unfortunately I've been involved in investigating stabbings in Cambridge, in Ely, in Cambourne and in other areas that nobody would ever expect to encounter that level or type of violence.

I've watched CCTV of a thirteen year old stabbing a fifteen year old in Cambridge City centre.

County Lines is absolutely about creating an honour system where these things are acceptable and you know that they're going to happen.

So if someone owes money for drugs – you know they're going to get stabbed or killed.

If you don't do something you are ordered to do as part of a County Lines gang, you know that you're going to be beaten up, or stabbed.

The violence is there because there is no other method of regulating the market for drugs – it's illegal. People can't go to the police if they get robbed. If someone owes money you can't sue them for it. So it falls back on violence and fear.

To be a successful and profitable drug runner you need to be feared *and you'll never be loved*. As soon as people start to love you they don't act scared any more. Kindness in any form is usually perceived as a personal weakness.

We talked before about our levels of personal and self-awareness increasing our levels of sympathy, empathy and compassion. There is no room for any of those feelings in this business model – and where they are found they get punished and stamped out. Those feelings literally stop you from making more profit – and there is only one thing that counts in the County Lines business plan – make as much money as you can.

Now all of this sounds pretty horrible – and it is – but the final part of the business plan is to make it look appealing and to make it seem cool and desirable.

People who get hooked into County Lines don't have a frank talk with the person they end up working for where they are open and honest about these things.

The person who persuades that young person to get involved in this lifestyle is a false friend. They get inside their head and they tell them lots of things that aren't true – *whatever they need to say to get that young person to behave in a certain way.*

This might involve giving them gifts, if it's a girl they might trick them into thinking that they are in love with them. It might include pretending to be business partners. It usually involves bringing that young person to lots of parties, getting drunk and doing drugs for the first time.

Doing drugs is always on the menu because if they can get you hooked on anything, then you are really dependent on them and you'll do whatever you are told.

Debt is another thing. Lending money, being owed money, doing favours – creates a responsibility to pay that back. Small favours done by County Lines dealers have to be repaid with big favours by you. Small loans have to be repaid two or three times over.

There are examples of people effectively working for dealers under debt slavery for months and never even knowing the dealer's real name.

The whole time – once that dealer gets you hooked in – they'll try to re-program your thinking so that you don't trust your real friends. Your teachers, the police, the people you have grown up with, your mum, dad or brother or sister. They want you isolated and so then if you get to a point where you really want to get out of this nightmare – you don't feel like you've got anyone you can turn to.

The teenage suicide rate in the UK is at a record high right now (September 2020) – and particularly with girls aged between 15 and 19. People only take their own life when they feel absolutely desperate and like they have no way out at all. This is exactly how a County Lines drug dealer wants you to feel.

Chapter Two: How do you fit into the County Lines model?

This is a chapter that really depends on who you are individually. A decent level of self-awareness is important when we consider this question.

Like a recruitment officer for the army, a County Lines runner will try to persuade you that there is a place for you in their organisation – no matter who you are.

They might see you as a customer, first and foremost. They want your cash.

If they can get you to buy weed – that's good – but it's no big deal. If you're like most young people you're not loaded with money (congrats to you if you are) so getting £10 together for weed is what it is. But for you that will add up if you end up smoking it three times a week with your friends (£30 per week, or £120 per month).

You might all end up chipping in a bit to afford it – but then people start watching who is smoking the most and it can get problematic.

It does add up. The County Lines guy will act like he's going to do you some favours – but there are no favours.

So your first place on the County Lines spectrum is as a customer and he (it usually is a he) wants to get inside your pocket and your wallet.

One £10 purchase is not enough for him because he's a greedy guy — so he'll persuade you to use more than you can pay for, and pay him back 'whenever'. Once you get into debt to him — that's when your relationship will change.

Either he gets quite intimidating and scary — and starts pressing you for that money (and you might feel like you need to clear that debt so quickly that you do something desperate to get that money) or he'll give you options on 'other ways' that you can pay it back.

If you're a girl this might include asking you to do sexual things for him or become his 'girlfriend'. This isn't about him respecting you or wanting to do the right thing by you — it's usually about testing your boundaries.

There is a thing called 'Child Sexual Exploitation' (or CSE). Creating a debt that is paid for 'in kind' means that young women — often younger than 16 — have some form of sex with men (sometimes the dealer — often not the dealer) to pay the debt.

What many of the girls who are exploited in this way never realise is that when they are introduced to men who they are effectively forced to perform sex acts on, that dealer is getting paid for introducing them. Usually he is getting paid much more than the debt – but he will keep telling the girl that she hasn't paid it off yet.

Alternatively, he might try to persuade the girl that this is a really easy way to support her use of cannabis or another drug that she is using. She gets to go to parties – he pays for her to get there – he might even gift her clothes so that she looks a certain way. All she has to do is 'be nice' to these men.

For a lot of these girls this is their first sexual experience – and it is a loveless and painful one that is degrading and humiliating. It will stay with them for the rest of their lives and they'll always struggle to look at men who are attracted to them for healthy and positive reasons, in a healthy and positive way.

This is what we call 'debt bondage'. When it comes to the time that you think you can walk away – you get told that you are not allowed to. That's when you start to feel trapped and we get into a situation that is called 'coercive behaviour'. This is a pretty fancy way of describing bullying and harassment – making people do things that they just don't want to do. Not little things, not minor things – but traumatic things.

When a girl is under 16 and she has sex or engages in sex acts it is illegal in the UK if the person she is with doesn't reasonably believe that she is 16 yet. The UK law doesn't consider a person – boy or girl – under 16, to be old enough to make a decision on that yet.

You might disagree with that very strongly – and I'm not here to argue with you – it's just where the law stands.

If you're not 16 and someone has penetrative sex with you knowing that you are not 16, you are a rape victim, and they are guilty of rape.

If you're not yet 12 it doesn't matter if the person knows whether you're under 16 or not. There is no defence to having sex with someone who is not yet 12. Nobody looks at an 11 year old and thinks they are 16.

The reason why the law is so careful about people under 16 having sex is because it is so easy to make a decision that you regret for the rest of your life. We call that trauma. You can easily feel traumatised by getting compromised sexually – and you are never more vulnerable than when you are engaged in a sexual behaviour, particularly so if you don't know or trust the person that you are with.

If that person has paid money to someone else to be with you — they have certain expectations. That might include them believing that they can do whatever they want to you, and that they can force you, use violence upon you, not use contraception or practise safe sex.

They might have STDs (sexually transmitted diseases) ranging from herpes or chlamydia all the way up to syphilis or even HIV/AIDs. *How would you ever know if they have those things?* The consequences can range from infertility, to burning pains — all the way up to life limiting illnesses and your immune system collapsing. HIV/AIDs is still a prominent killer — it is more manageable than it once was, but there is no cure.

All this is because this guy has 'given' you some weed. It is very easy to get backed into a corner at a party and be put in a position where you can't say no (even if you didn't owe the guy any money).

This is not to say that the same can't happen to boys — because there is a market to abuse boys sexually too — but we know that it is far more likely to happen to girls.

When it does happen it can involve human trafficking and modern day slavery offences.

Basically this means that a child or young person (under 18) is taken from their home town and they are sent to another area to attend these parties or to go and be involved in this type of activity.

It's a crime for anyone to arrange this to happen. If a young person is subjected to that type of trafficking – *even if they think they want to go* (and it might be in a train, in a car, via a taxi – whatever) it's still a crime. If a young person commits a crime because they felt like they had to while they were being trafficked – they have a defence in law because they had little choice in the matter.

So this part takes you from being a customer to becoming an exploited young person and a victim. We call it child exploitation but it covers anyone up to the age 18 including young people and teenagers.

Another situation doesn't involve sexual exploitation – it just involves getting you to be comfortable with handling bigger quantities of drugs and become part of the supply chain.

So you want some weed – and they'll give you what you want, if you carry this package from here to there. To begin with it might even be an empty box just to test you and get you comfortable – they want to see that you're reliable. All you're doing is dropping off a box, a bag or a flask or something like that at a particular address. You don't have to handle any money – just drop it off.

That doesn't feel so hard – and a bit of 'free' weed is cool. From there the tasks might get a bit more demanding – or the rewards might be more tempting.

That might include carrying cash now, it might include hiding drugs around your parent's house, and it might involve you becoming a rider, on your bike or moped delivering at different times of night with little warning.

As you do this you won't get caught straight away and you could feel really weird and worried about it to begin with. But as you 'get away with it' you start to feel untouchable – nothing is going wrong – and you're getting rewarded, so you're getting comfortable and confident.

There is a thing that is called your 'comfort zone' – anything inside this is what you're happy with, the things that you do for the first time and make you feel awkward and self-conscious or embarrassed or anxious – those things are outside of your comfort zone.

For many people getting up in front of a lot of people and talking about something makes them feel really vulnerable and embarrassed. Until you've done it many times, you don't get confident with it. The more you do it, the better you get at it, and the more comfortable you become. Suddenly doing public speaking is inside your comfort zone.

If you've been riding around town with drugs on you – even riding past the police and they didn't notice or stop you – you get comfortable, and you take it for granted and it's cool. You're also getting rewarded – either some payment, gifts or drugs.

That's all fine – *until it gets out of your control.*

As you get known, you start to get identified – not only by the police but by other drug dealers and customers. You're carrying something they want – either cash or drugs – and how are you going to go to the police and tell them that you got robbed of your drugs and drug money? How are you going to tell your dealer that you got stopped by the police?

We'll come back to that in a bit.

When I was working in York, I worked out of a police station on Fulford Road. One day we had a man who came into the enquiry office and put a bag of white power down on the desk.

Initially we thought he'd found some drugs and was handing them in – which would have been fine – no crime there.

Instead he told us:

"I just bought this bag of coke off a dealer – and it's not coke at all, it's definitely amphet [amphetamine powder] and I want him arrested because he ripped me off"

Genuinely. This happened. We were so amazed by how bizarre this was that my colleague went through and got the sergeant and told him. The bloke making the complaint was arrested for attempting to possess a class A drug (cocaine) and was taken through to custody.

It was one of the strangest things I've ever seen.

People in the drugs market set each other up and rip each other off all the time – they have no way to ask the police to intervene. That's why people say "There's no honour amongst thieves" – what they mean to say is, that no matter how much people claim there are honour codes outside of the law, there aren't, and people outside of the law have no protection from being ripped off.

So this scenario has you effectively working for a dealer but getting drawn into increasing amounts of risk, for what seems like more reward, but you probably won't stop to ask yourself – in the long term – if the rewards are actually worth it.

This is where we come back to self-awareness and knowledge of self. If you're in touch with what you really want from your life you'll have something to compare these offers to – to decide whether drug dealing is better than the plan that you have for yourself, or if it's just going to stop you getting there.

For most people it just side-tracks them into a place where the risks are getting bigger and bigger – and the rewards are beginning to look less and less worth it. This is particularly true if the reward never arrives or never quite gets delivered in the way that you think it ought to be.

A lot of the time the small amounts of money that you get rewarded with are easily spent and you forget what you did with it.

The big rewards only come with the big risks – this might include travelling down to London on the train, meeting a total stranger, and carrying a kilo of drugs back up to wherever you came from. Or if you live in London, being sent out of your familiar area, loaded up with drugs, to hand off to somebody you don't even know.

That is an utterly insane amount of risk.

You have to trust that the bag is actually right — weighs correctly — and contains what you were supposed to deliver, because if you get back to your area and some drugs are missing, or the cash isn't right, you're the first one to get the blame.

This is how easily young people end up in trafficking drugs though — is escalates pretty quickly. You might be expected to swallow condoms and plastic bags containing drugs to hide them from the police — and then pick them out of your poo when they get to the other end. You might have to take laxatives to get them out, and there's always the risk that a plastic bag or a condom could burst delivering a lethal dose of cocaine, heroin, MDMA or some other substance.

If you're a big lad or you're just known for being particularly aggressive or hard — and you're not scared of getting into a confrontation or a fight — you might be included just as someone who is ready to be rewarded for doing something desperate to someone else. Being involved in a gang can involve beating, stabbing someone, intimidating them, collecting debts — all these things need doing and throughout history organised crime groups have always sought out people willing to help them to do this dirty work.

Your part in this could be doing all those things. As with running drugs from point A to point B we are talking about getting inside your comfort zone.

"Just go along with Henry stand behind him and look nasty. Watch his back, and if the guy plays up just show him the knife."

I've known young people given weapons including imitation firearms, to use to intimidate people. One young man that I prosecuted received a substantial extra length of time on his prison sentence because he had an imitation firearm that had been converted to fire rounds.

We sent the weapon off to a special ballistics lab which included a firing range. It was tested professionally and they gave us a report about the capability of the weapon to kill people (it could).

This young man explained to me that it began with his handler telling him *"Just wave the gun about to scare them – shout at them – act like you're ready to use it"*.

In reality he was deeply uncomfortable and was scared that when he produced the gun, someone else would produce a gun, and he'd be the one ending up being shot. Or someone might take it off him and shoot him.

With escalating violence it usually gets out of your control. People react in unpredictable ways and you can't really say what someone is going to do if you threaten them with a knife, an imitation firearm or a firearm.

In addition to that, police responses to reports of anyone being seen with a weapon like that are quite hard line – usually it will involve a specialist unit like a dog unit or a firearms unit being deployed. Even if you're only 14 or 15 years old – until the weapon has been recovered and is out of the picture – the risks to you (of serious injury) are very high.

A County Lines' gang will try to recruit people who are comfortable to carry drugs, cash, and defend those things with physical force – including the use of weapons.

If they think that you can be persuaded to do that – for a limited period of time - you will be exactly what they're looking for. One step at a time they will take you through a process that we call 'indoctrination' – this is a process of influence upon your thoughts and your decision making. They will try to get your thinking to resemble theirs — so that your reactions are the same as theirs would be. This is so that you can justify your actions to yourself — no matter how ugly, criminal or harmful those actions might be

Ultimately they want you to value nobody or anything any higher than your relationship with their gang or group.

This can happen in a couple of different ways — either they succeed in getting inside your head and persuading you that your life is in this now, and that you've taken this criminal lifestyle on. Alternatively they get you far enough in to be terrified of them so that you don't think there is any way you can get out — and that possibly they might even kill you if you tried.

Ideally though — if they can do it by converting you and indoctrinating you — you'll start to resemble someone who has been 'radicalised'. You might recognise this phrase from the TV as it is often used in connection to terrorism. When someone is so convinced of their membership to a cause, a religion, or a purpose — they might even be ready to give their lives to it.

That's the kind of loyalty that organised crime wants. That you'll never talk about them or snitch. You'll never back anyone before them — no matter if they are right or wrong — and you can be trusted in any circumstances to put the gang first and yourself second. They want you to look at the gang as your family – as a bond that is stronger than blood – and a commitment that is more important to you than anything else in the whole world.

Part and parcel of this is making you feel bad about yourself. They can persuade you that you have nothing to offer to the world – that you can't make it on your own, that you can't make it legitimately, that your dreams are silly and unrealistic – so you have little or no option. If you want to be something more than nothing, you have to commit yourself to what *they do* and what they offer you.

No criminal gang ever made it from telling their gang members to follow their dreams and be a huge success for themselves.

So your place to begin with – no matter what – is at the bottom of the whole pecking order.

Every single person in that gang is above you, and there is no value in ever introducing you to anyone else – so in all likelihood the most senior person you will meet or speak to will be your handler.

Although you will be asked for absolute obedience and reliability – being at the bottom of the pecking order means that you have to put up with a complete double standard in reply. They don't owe you the same loyalty or faithful amount of commitment. You are there to run for them, do as you are told, and take whatever rewards are offered. You're not in a position to negotiate, haggle or ask for more.

They didn't select you to be ambitious – they chose you to get this from here to there, to collect some money reliably, and be in a certain place at a certain time (no matter what time of day or night that might be).

This leads on to your next place in the whole scheme of things.

Everybody knows Biggie Smalls or the Notorious B.I.G. – he's like a founding father of rap music and an immortal icon of the whole hip-hop movement. He's another rapper – like Jay-Z – who started out in selling crack cocaine in New York.

He wrote a song called *'The Ten Crack Commandments'*. So it's obviously like the 'ten commandments' in the Bible – the rules that God gave to Moses to deliver to his people to guide them on how they should live – but in *this* ten commandments Biggie is telling people the rules about being a drug dealer.

What did he say was rule number 8?

*"Number 8, never keep weight on you
Them cats that squeeze guns can hold jums too"*

Don't know what that means? Ok well this song came out in 1997 – so the slang is maybe a bit dated. But basically Biggie is saying if you don't carry the drugs it's hard to prove you had anything to do with them. You won't get mugged, you won't get arrested, you won't get prosecuted – if the drugs aren't on you.

So the County Lines' guys – they don't want to carry those drugs and that risk. If they can get you to do it, and they can rely on you with it – they're not going to get caught or prosecuted (in the worst case scenario, you will, they don't care).

Your place is to hold that risk. Have those drugs on you or hidden in your parent's house – along with the cash and anything else that should incriminate them.

They are protected by using you as a shield. You might think – *they might have persuaded you by now to think* - that they would never give you up. Truth be told this is so that you would never give them up. They can rely on you – after you've been arrested – to never snitch, identify or do anything that would harm them.

If there is a prison sentence coming you need to believe that it will be for you in these circumstances and not for them – and they're not going to visit you because they're already recruiting the next person to fill your shoes.

Now – what they want you to see as your place in the County Lines model is as a streetwise person – young man or young woman – who is urban and cool. You're well dressed, have some money, have some weed when you want it, you can hook your friends up with what they need, and you don't depend on anyone to say yes or no.

They want you to see County Lines as a fast route to the better things in life – and they want to define those 'better things' as material objects, like mobile phones, fashionable trainers, tracksuits, clothing, jewellery – designer gear.

They'll let you hold onto money so that you like the feel of it – *but it won't be your money*, you can just fall in love with it. They'll want you to get hooked on parties with strangers, and mixing with a much older crowd.

They will expose you to experiences that you're not ready for – but in an exciting way that you can't back out of. They will make the world seem suddenly alive – but chaotic – and they want you to feel like you're achieving all the time, and that this is what success feels like. There's a certain amount of adrenaline involved – and that does *feel* good, but that's the difference between perception and reality. They thrive and succeed when they get you to accept a version of reality that is absolutely false.

Only people who have real self-knowledge and understanding can actually tell the difference and see through this stuff – *knowing what they need and what they don't need.*

The great Malcolm X – the American civil rights leader – went through several stages of radicalisation in his life. He wrote about in his autobiography and I recommend that you read it.

His first radicalisation was criminal. He was scooped up off the streets in exactly the way that I have just described. Of course, he ended up in prison and on the run from someone who wanted to kill him.

His second radicalisation was religious and political – when he was indoctrinated by the Nation of Islam. Later in his life his study and his self-awareness grew and he recognised that neither was very much better than the other – and both embraced violence as a means to their ends.

In the third and final stage of his life – when he really achieved his personal sense of self-awareness and knowledge he converted to orthodox Islam and embraced it as a religion of peace. He said:

> *"A man who stands for nothing will fall for anything"*

Chapter Three: What are the risks posed to you?

I'm not scared to tell you the truth. We will talk in language that is plain and simple and we will not flinch from things that are awkward or difficult to address in this chapter.

There's a lot that can happen to you when you get wrapped up in County Lines. I've heard it explained to me as being in a living nightmare — and that's from someone who did get out the other side of it relatively 'OK' (few do).

Criminal Prosecution

Ok — so criminal prosecution has to be up there right? If you get caught carrying drugs, cash, scales, and your mobile phone is full of orders for this or that amount of 'brown' (heroin) or 'white' (cocaine) — you're looking at possession with intent to supply or at the very least possession.

A criminal prosecution for possession of a controlled drug — or possession with intent to supply (PWITS) is a real dead-end for your future career.

If you've got ambition to get a job in any type of role which we'd describe as 'a position of trust' —

virtually anything with some level of responsibility (and let's be honest, anything interesting) – having to answer questions at the interview stage about having a drugs conviction is not a cool place to be. That's if you get an interview.

The truth is, it hands an immediate advantage to other people competing against you for that internship, that apprenticeship, that place at University or that job that you really wanted.

In addition we're moving into a whole new world now – Brexit is going to be in effect and we won't have freedom of movement across Europe.

Drugs convictions already have to be declared if you want to apply for a visa to visit several international destinations (Australia, the United States and Canada being three popular examples) – having a drug conviction, or worse a conviction for dealing – will certain stop you from getting to visit some pretty amazing places.

I've been to Canada and America and I count myself lucky because both were amazing trips. I have a clear history and nothing to declare and it means a lot to me. I'd like to go to Australia or New Zealand, I have friends living in Sidney and I definitely intend to visit them.

Now, more than ever, having a clean personal history is really important. You might want to work in the technology sector – imagine being offered that dream job at Google or Microsoft, in California or Seattle – but not being able to get that work permit that you need. That would be horrendous.

Imagine being a talented athlete and not being able to compete. A model that can't do a foreign photoshoot. Perhaps you want to study abroad?

We kind of take all of these things for granted because for years we have been in the EU (and during that time we could just move to Germany, France, Italy, Spain or wherever) and our passports have always been strong enough for us to have a really great chance to just do this stuff with countries outside of the EU zone. More than ever it's about you and your ability as an individual to persuade that country to accept you (something you can't take for granted). A history of criminality won't be looked at with any degree of sympathy – they just don't want to know (why should they?).

Receiving a criminal prosecution – or the equivalent to a criminal prosecution (which includes a traditional caution, youth caution or conditional caution) is a real barrier to employment and travel – but you might be more worried about the immediate effects that come along with criminal prosecution.

In and of itself getting prosecuted does tend to become a self-fulfilling prophecy. You're a convicted offender now – so getting a good job gets harder, the hardship that you suffer makes the money you might gain from drug dealing more attractive, you might feel more drawn to drugs as a method of escape – so you can end up sinking into this part of society and it's actually pretty easily done. Sinking in is one thing, but climbing back out is much, much harder.

From that point on you're trying to get a second chance – get someone to invest some trust and faith in you – get off that minimum wage, and have someone go out on a limb for you and defy the expectations that you're about to do something seriously wrong at any moment.

I'll be honest with you – as a young person you will be given much more leniency or sympathy than any adult. When you become an adult and reach 18 you have a much better chance to turn around and say "I got into some trouble growing up – but I'm a lot more mature now, and I've changed". That frankly doesn't work for someone who is 35 and was convicted of burglary last year – "Well I'm not 34 anymore and it's been a big change", that just doesn't work in the same way.

The idea of the Youth Justice system is to give young people the chance to make mistakes and to be forgiven for those mistakes – what the 'hang over' from such a mistake is depends largely on how significant the crime was.

Possession of cannabis is something that we can overcome and rehabilitate a reputation from and you'll find that lots of people want to support you and help you with the issues that led to that mistake. You can work hard and find an opportunity to demonstrate that things have changed.

Something more worrying is on the other end of the scale – like being caught on school premises with a volume of class A drugs, or a quantity of MDMA tablets for example – would take a lot more work to redeem yourself from.

There are structures in place to help you cope with minor and low-end mistakes that break the law. The system is geared to try and be supportive and not give a criminal history to someone without a real need to do that.

People who need to be recorded with a criminal history are obviously people who are going to go on and commit more offences or worse offences. This is so that people in public can be protected from the effects of their behaviour and choices.

Being marked as someone who is a 'threat to society' is a deeply unpleasant thing. In and of itself being alienated from your community and known as someone who spreads harm — by supplying drugs, through violent or intimidating behaviours — all of these things are actually quite traumatic. In your private moments you'd probably sit and look at yourself and say *"How did I end up here — I'm none of these things really"*.

Sexual Exploitation

We've actually looked in a bit of detail about how sexual exploitation can happen. What we haven't really talked about is what sexual exploitation causes and how harmful it really is.

It's very harmful and traumatic for both boys and girls. People of any type of gender identity can be harmed through the sexual exploitation of children. In the most frank way — and it's a really ugly thought — criminal gangs don't care what your gender is, what your sexual identity is, or how you define yourself. Broadly speaking — if you're a girl and they can exploit you for sexual gain by effectively selling you or a sex act that you could perform on a man or a woman — the money is what they are interested in. The same is absolutely true of a boy, girl or anyone. If they have to drug you to gain compliance, a criminal gang would not be above doing that to loosen your inhibitions. A whole range of drugs from MDMA to Rohypnol (Flunitrazepam – a hypnotic) can easily be disguised in a drink and once administered can be used to overcome resistance on both a physical and psychological level.

Very often the aftermath of a forced or coercive sexual encounter is the worst part. Living with yourself and coming to terms with what happened can be incredibly difficult – you've suffered trauma, and managing a trauma takes expert support and help. Sometimes medication will help to keep you calm and to work through anxiety, flash backs and panic attacks.

A number of young people suffering this type of mistreatment throw themselves towards drugs in an effort to 'self-medicate' – they find that drink or drugs helps the negative emotions to go away, they forget for a while – and a really unhealthy cycle of self-abuse, regret and even self-harm (such as eating disorders or cutting[1]) can start to come in.

Aside from that – being abused on a sexual level begins to redefine your self-identity.

---

[1] Harming yourself with a blade or sharp object;

We talked earlier about your 'comfort zone' – and getting used to new experiences. No matter what – being sold to an adult stranger that you don't know, have no idea how old they are – and who has an expectation to be allowed to treat you exactly as they please and without any measure of respect or dignity – this is never going to be 'ok' with your comfort zone.

Sadly though, sexual exploitation does terrible things to your opinion of yourself. A person who has been raped looks at themselves and questions why it happened to them – they might desperately try to wash it away in the bath or shower. They find that nothing will get rid of the mark that it leaves on them. They always have a knowledge of the day they were raped, how it happened, where and when. No matter how desperate they are, they cannot go back and do that day over again and not go through that experience. For someone who is subjected to sexual exploitation, it is that – but multiple times over, with different people, and you begin to look upon yourself as a second class person. Most girls or boys of your age don't have to go through that. They aren't regularly subjected to that. They don't offer themselves to it – *but you blame yourself and you start to think that is what you are worth.*

It is not what you are worth – it never will be what you are worth – and if an adult pressures you and manipulates you and guides you into a sexually exploitative position, *that is about them committing crimes against you.* Deeply dehumanising and degrading crimes – and they should be brought to justice for doing that.

No matter how much justice follows – and people are prosecuted for the sexual exploitation of children – it won't make the hurt, the harm or the trauma go away. It will help to validate you, and it helps you to rebuild, but you tend to be rebuilding from a position where you feel absolutely ruined and you don't know how you will ever really piece together a healthy functioning relationship with someone you truly want to have in your life.

The person doing the exploitation and trafficking will always say "It will be fine" or "You'll have a good time" – but as soon as you put yourself on the train, or in that taxi, or allow them to drive you to that party absolutely nobody there is preoccupied with whether or not you actually are 'fine' or whether you have a good time.

The organised criminal gang is concerned with making money. The person who is using you is entirely focused on whether they get what they want for the money that they have paid. You will not know, and you'll play no part in any agreement that is reached towards that. You are an absolute non-human in that context.

We talked earlier about the development of pity, leading to sympathy, leading to empathy, leading to compassion. The people who abuse children and young people for money — and will pay people for the opportunity to inflict sexual harm on children and young people - will not be operating beyond the boundaries of pity (few operate within the boundaries of pity). Any person with an ounce of sympathy — when confronted with a vulnerable young person who has been pressured into an illegal sexual transaction of this nature – could not go through with it. Consequently you have to be incredibly aware that this person is probably capable of deeply cruel behaviours, and that is an enormously dangerous place to be.

As a result, sexual exploitation and the physical harm of a child or young person — sometimes talked about in misleading terms like "rough sex" can include the making of indecent imagery (photos and video) that can also be distributed for profit. There is a huge market on the dark web which is also very profitable for circles of paedophiles and people with abusive tendencies who want to see very dark and harmful things. No young person under the age of 18 can consent to be involved in this type of thing – although the people who make and manufacture and distribute such content describe it as 'child pornography'. What the police refer to – absolutely exclusively – is indecent imagery of children and crime scene imagery.

On the most factual basis – these type of experiences break people – and very sadly I have seen and met young people who have taken their own lives or went on to commit suicide as a result of sexual abuse.

Violence

County Lines activity creates violent subcultures that young people are scared to speak out about. The fear of violence in our communities cannot ever be a good thing. Seeing people encourage greater levels of violence towards young people and vulnerable people is horrendous.

Writing for you and to you – I want so much better for you than that.

I've already mentioned the CCTV that I had to view as a police officer where a 13 year old boy stabbed a 15 year old boy. The offence was committed swiftly and almost casually. The victim had been fighting in a street, the camera was just above them looking down — it was like watching out of a window from across the road.

The 15 year old boy ended up on the floor and as one offender was punching him, the offender with the knife ran up, and, having glanced up the road, stabbed him once in the lower leg. The sharp knife easily penetrated the skin and was drawn back out again in one swift movement.

The victim was hospitalised and required stitches. The mental and emotional trauma and fear that he suffered was far greater and was very difficult to come to terms with.

I know other victims of serious violence — who have been stabbed — who cannot cope in public anymore. They have turned to the same pattern of 'self-medication' — seeking an answer to their anxiety through smoking weed or drinking alcohol.

Being stabbed is another example of behaviour that robs someone of their humanity. We all have a right to our bodies not being violated. We've talked about sexual harm and how that violates our mental, emotional and physical boundaries — but knife crime actually operates in a very similar way.

The victim feels powerless. They've been robbed of their right not to be treated in this way – they suffer emotional frustration, anger, a desire for revenge, fear, sensations of guilt – and other confusing and conflicting psychological and emotional experiences that they just don't know how to cope with.

Unlike the act of a sexual abuser – where many of the abusers never feel a sense of remorse or guilt – for a lot of young people who are talked into picking up a knife and using it against someone – stabbing someone is also dehumanising for them too.

Making yourself into the sort of person who can actually disregard the social boundaries and expectations, silence the inner voice that is telling you not to do something like that, and driving yourself on to put a knife into someone – you're pressing yourself into a mental condition that is harmful and is likely to play and repeat in flashbacks and dreams time and time and time again.

Once that is burned into your psyche, and once it's there in your mental loop – there's no effective way to de-programme that.

People coming back from war zones where they are paid to fight and kill often return home quite unlike the person that went out to that conflict.

Their loved ones talk about the distance that now exists, staring into space, being there but not being there – how numb they seem.

People with post-traumatic stress disorder talk about being present when a miraculous life changing event has happened to them – but not being able to feel it when it does. For example – the birth of a baby – feeling disconnected from the birth of your first child.

Being a person who engaged in extreme levels of violence – and who may have suffered severe violence – takes you to a very dark place. In this dark place you battle psychologically and emotionally with your own sense of guilt and shame. You may suffer depression. You criticise yourself. If nobody else ever knows what you have done – if they never find out that it was you – you still have to live with that.

People with horrendous criminal histories who meet people that they form an emotional connection to always have to overcome the moment when they reveal who they are to that person. They are always worried about it. *"Will they be disgusted? Will they walk away from me?*

If they stay, might I end up being violent towards them?"

Bringing violence into your life (and the fundamental foundation of how County Lines is ruled and controlled is through violence and fear) you bring something incredibly complicated and very toxic into your world. It's hard to carry on afterwards – you lose something that you can never get back.

Additionally, when you personally reset your tolerance of violence to a different (higher) level – your reactions change. It's difficult to function in society when you've done that. Something like walking down the street becomes a more intimidating experience. The hostility that you perceive around yourself at all times is turned up – like the volume is set higher. You go into a pub or a public meeting space – and someone acts out in a certain way, maybe in a joke, maybe it has nothing to do with you – and you feel targeted by it, you feel immediately on edge, and you have this irrational and instinctive reaction to do something about it...

Cycles of violence are very difficult to escape from or to recondition yourself after. Again – self-knowledge and understanding helps a great deal – but if you have taken yourself to a place where these things are a part of you now, it's very unlikely that you can do that alone. You need professional help and assistance to rehabilitate and get you back to a healthier way of being.

When people advise to walk away from confrontations – it's not to help the other person you might otherwise attack or hurt – *it's to help you*. So you never have to sit in that position where you're saying to yourself *"Why did I have to do that?"*

Perhaps the oldest piece of advice about welcoming violence into your life is the saying that "Those who live by the sword, die by the sword" – a saying that has survived hundreds of years and originated in the bible.

Drug Abuse

I've really chosen just a handful of the major risks associated with County Lines – there are so many genuine risks involved. The final risk that I want to highlight might seem like the most obvious one: drug abuse.

Drug abuse can range from prescription medication all the way up to crack cocaine addiction.

Basically, if you think you need help on a medicated level the conversation to have is with a doctor, a nurse, a mental health specialist or a qualified person who operates in the relevant field of concern (a clinician). This is what we call 'objective advice'.

'Subjective advice' is what you might come up with based on the information available to you – which might be quite limited. Whatever that subjective advice is, you tend to apply an interpretation to it that is about *what you'd like the outcome to be.*

It's like when you do a 'pick a hand' thing (in one hand is something you want, in the other hand is something you don't want). When you pick the thing you didn't want, you give in to yourself and let yourself pick again. Inevitably you find a way to justify the choice that you wanted to make in the first place and you 'cheat'. With another person there – it's harder to do that.

Drug reward and dependency is really like this. Particularly if you've already tried the drug and you really liked what it did for you in that moment.

Channel 4 had a controlled experiment ('Drugs Live'[2]) where they administered certain

---

[2]

https://www.youtube.com/watch?v=mmhWZPwVUNM

controlled drugs to members of the public (MDMA and Cannabis). All of the drugs were checked and the volumes were considered to be safe. There was no dangerous impurity involved and doctors were on standby to deal with any unexpected outcomes.

A member of the clergy was introduced to MDMA / ecstasy and she really got a big kick out of it that she described as 'euphoria'. Euphoria is a state of absolute bliss – it's a combination of being at peace, but being incredibly happy at the same time. People who describe 'euphoria' talk about a sense of glowing happiness and feeling of confidence, that is accompanied by a sense of warmth and love, and being loved. Her praise for the experience was strong enough to believe that she might chose to experiment with MDMA again.

For that particular lady her subjective assessment – her recollection of the drug that she took – was very positive, but it was her own assessment and that made it 'subjective'. It was related to her own experience alone.

An objective position would be one where professional clinicians or doctors talked to her about the up-side and the down-side with her in comparison to other people and the result of that conversation would be 'objective'. An 'objective' assessment is a much stronger one – and is more logical and not as likely to be influenced by craving or symptoms of addiction or feelings of pleasure and enjoyment.

When people self-medicate it is usually coming from a *subjective* assessment of what they feel they need to do to improve their lives. They might not feel like something was missing from their lives until they get involved in drugs – but drugs can be like that – they can make you feel like you needed this experience all along.

For people who feel inhibited (that is they're really shy and they struggle to talk to other people or join in with things going on around them) a drug can be something that gives them confidence. This includes drinking alcohol – which also lowers inhibitions and makes people feel more outgoing. Cannabis tends to make people care less about what other people feel or think – or might give a false sense that everyone is hooked into the same collective vibe together (particularly if they are smoking the weed as a group). MDMA (ecstasy) is a party drug that can give people that 'loved up' feeling – offering affection to total strangers, and there are lots of stories about becoming sexually more permissive and doing things in a sexual way that they later struggle to understand or don't feel happy they did.

Getting into drug abuse is about finding a quick fix between where you currently are — towards feeling how you'd prefer to feel under the best circumstances. Cocaine will make you feel like you've won a gold medal at the Olympics for absolutely no reason whatsoever. People who take cocaine feel incredibly over-confident about themselves and have fantastic self-opinion. Nothing has actually changed in their life — they've just hit their brain with a certain type of stimulant, and it has tricked them mentally into thinking that everything is fantastic.

Cocaine lifts you up almost immediately (particularly crack cocaine) — but it can drop out without any warning after twenty minutes leaving you looking for another hit.

Crack cocaine has a shorter cycle — it takes less time to hit your brain, and the hit itself lasts for even less time — maybe ten minutes.

After using cocaine people usually feel really down and hung over — they can start feeling anxious and paranoid. A state of paranoia is where you are convinced that things are wrong when they're actually probably fine (which is the complete opposite of how you'll feel when you're high on cocaine).

Getting involved in drug abuse is the clearest indication of all that you have an unhappiness in your life that you do need to tackle. Most drugs are a *masking* agent – they help you to carry on and ignore your problems – they are the opposite of self-awareness or personal knowledge.

The only way to really take yourself to a place of genuine happiness is to get to know yourself – identify what is that you really want to be – and to make a long term plan that helps you to set about achieving it. No matter what that goal or objective is – you can get there. You might not have that self-belief, but as you take small steps towards your goal, you learn to believe in yourself and what you can achieve. You realise that you don't need a chemical to lie to your brain – and you don't need violent drug suppliers in your life demanding money (or worse) in return for that feeling of achievement and success, that calm that you are seeking, of being at peace with yourself.

At the end of this book I will provide you with some very important resources that will help you to cope if you are already struggling with issues to do with using drugs or feeling drug dependent. *And yes – cannabis does create dependency issues – so if someone has told you that you can't get hooked on weed, that person is not telling you the truth or they don't know enough about drugs to be giving you advice.*

Chapter Four: How do you get your life back?

I'm writing this chapter for anyone who is feeling desperate – who recognises the experiences that we've already talked about, and is starting to feel (either because of this book or simply just because they've been going down that road for a while) that they need to get out of a difficult and traumatic position that they have found themselves in.

First of all let me get one thing straight.

I know that you probably feel one way on one day, and that you feel the other way the next. You might feel *both* ready to get of County Lines or drugs and also like you just don't want to give it up – both things conflicting and arguing inside you at the same time.

This doesn't make you 'crazy'.

I'm not judging you because you got drawn into such a difficult position. Maybe you're just on the fringes of it and you've seen enough but you don't know how to turn back now. Either way – I don't blame you for where you are. What's really important is that we get you the help that you need to make sense of your thoughts and feelings, and you can make the choices that you feel really positive about.

Somewhere in there is a conflicted person – you must like something about the lifestyle choices you made at some stage. While I don't judge you, and I don't blame you – I don't absolve you of the choices that you made. You made those choices and you now find yourself where you are.

That might sound pretty harsh – but look at it this way – if you make different choices, you can be somewhere else. So look how powerful your choices are.

All the way through this book I have encouraged you to look at yourself – evaluate and judge for yourself what you are proud of and what you genuinely think has been good and bad in your life.

It's only through your sense of self-knowledge that you can understand the lessons that those negative experiences have offered to you. Look at the mistakes as lessons – we all make mistakes in life – we all learn from the mistakes, or we ought to try to.

Even our heroes have flaws. It doesn't matter who you are a big fan of – *and it is good to have a hero that you look up to* – but that person will have made mistakes and done things wrong in their life too.

I was (am) a huge fan of Mohammed Ali growing up – and I read a lot about him. As I got beyond the usual fan adulation and the people who only want to say nice things and praise him – I found evidence that as well as being a civil rights icon, he was racist, and he bullied and taunted others through racist insults and abuse. *If you don't believe me read books or watch documentaries about his relationship with the boxer and his career long rival 'Smokin' Joe Frazier who he smeared as a 'gorilla' and an 'ugly negro'.*

We all let ourselves down from time to time, and finding the strength to forgive ourselves for our mistakes does lead us to finding more kindness for the people around us. We learn the lessons of sympathy, empathy and compassion.

When we see someone who is sleeping in a doorway, or someone who is making a mistake that we've made in the past – we're more likely to try to understand – we're more likely to try to do something helpful.

To begin with – getting your life back is about reclaiming your sense of identity, a knowledge of who you really are, and from there building a vision about the person you really want to become.

I don't think anything hurts quite as much – *once you form that vision of who you want to be* – as not measuring up to it. When people look at you in a way that says that you're not good enough to be that person – it hurts inside. If you tell someone your dream and they laugh at you – it hurts.

Both negative and positive emotions can be used to fuel your improvement.

Being motivated by a negative emotion is called an 'away from' motivator because it pushes you away from something you don't want to happen or avoids a negative outcome.

"I don't want to get out of bed this morning, but if I don't I'll lose my job, and I don't want to lose my job, so I'll get out of bed."

Sometimes that is called a 'disincentive'.

Being motivated by a positive emotion is called a 'towards motivator' – because you want to get there. You've been told that if you get a certain grade on the next test you're going to get that new pair of trainers that you really, really like – so you're going to study hard. Sometimes this is called an 'incentive'.

Whatever your current situation is – you need to identify your motivators – whether they are positive (incentives) or 'away from' factors.

So the first thing I want you to do is make an agreement with yourself: you're going to live your life with a greater sense of purpose – understanding what motivates you.

"I am not what I want to be right now. I don't like some fairly important things in my life right now. I want to do something about it."

In my life I want to be [*write down what you really want – you don't have to tell anyone, and even as I write this book, I will never know what you write here*]:

These are all the things I don't like and that I want to change [*write them all down and be really honest with yourself – use another piece of paper and staple it into the book if you need to*]:

These are all the things that I want to have more of in my life – these are the things that I think are more important than anything [*write them all down, stick pictures in the book if you can, draw things, colour them in – make them vivid and bold*]:

This might be the scariest and most challenging thing you've done in a long time – and you might feel 'silly' doing it. You might choose to skip over this bit and come back to it when you've thought about it for many days or even weeks. <u>That's up to you. This is your book and this for you to decide – nobody else.</u> I'm just happy for you if you can do it.

What do you think is your biggest problem right now? What do you think is the thing that is standing in your way?

When you decide what that thing is, you really need a mentor to help you to over-come that barrier. This needs to be someone that you can trust.

I appreciate that finding that trust – particularly if you've been through drug abuse, or exploitation, or you feel under threat from someone who is forcing you to do things – *that's incredibly difficult*. I really do understand that. Finding the strength to take someone into your confidence and trust again is the first step towards defying everything that you have been taught to believe in through the County Lines system.

This is where I ask you to do something very profound (which means something incredibly difficult, meaningful and important). It's life changing actually. *I'm going to ask you to trust me right now.*

If you feel under threat from someone, if you are tied up in a relationship with someone who is coercive (bullying), who makes you do things that leaves you feeling very unhappy – who you feel that you can't walk away from – you need to go to the person that you want to be your mentor, and you need to explain that you've read this book, that you recognise the problems, the issue and the trauma that's inside it. Finding the words is going to be really hard. **So say this to them:**

"Please, I need your help. I've got myself into a situation that I can't sort out on my own. I've looked at everyone that I know. I think you are the best person to help me right now. Please will you help me?"

Look in the mirror and practise saying that out loud.

From the knowledge I've gained from the people I've worked with, who have become wrapped up in the County Lines machinery, and those who have come so close to it that they have been hurt and traumatised by it, thinking about the young people I know who have self- medicated for one reason or another – I absolutely know that you will read that, and you will think *"There is absolutely no way that I will ever be able to do that"*.

You need to understand that there is a strength that is inside you that you don't know about yet. I know it is there – you don't know it is there yet – **it is there**. Yes, this is a terrifying thing to confront – but if you sit and think about it for long enough you will realise that this is only words. A series of sounds that come out of your mouth – you've been doing this since you were baby – you can do this. You don't think about it, you look down at the words, you say the words, and then the help that you need will arrive.

Nobody expects you to put your life back together all on your own. Nobody. Nobody will judge you for holding out your hand and asking for the help that you need to get you there. Doing this doesn't mean that it's someone else's achievement. For every medal winner, for every champion, for success story – there is a coach and a mentor and someone who didn't stop believing even at the time when that champion had given up on themselves. You are the only champion in this book.

Appreciate that you are not perfect – and nobody ever needs you to be perfect. Not at any moment in your life will you be judged against perfection – it's a false concept that doesn't exist. We trick ourselves into believing in perfection. You arrive in the world with a unique quality, and a personality that is all about you. All anyone will ever ask of you is that you make the most of that.

For professionals who get to work with young people it is a huge privilege – a massive event – to be asked to help someone when they really need it.

If you go to that person that you identified (your mentor) – and you tell them that you want them to be your mentor, that you need help, and that you want to improve and change – you will give them a gift that is more valuable than anything. Nobody can give them a bigger compliment than that.

I refuse to believe that they won't respond to it.

I recommend that you choose someone at school – a teacher or a pastoral care leader – someone who you look at and recognise as someone who has demonstrated sympathy, empathy, and compassion.

You might feel incredibly vulnerable and very shy about doing something like this. You might reflect on your past behaviours and remember a time when you weren't nice to that person – and you might think "They won't forgive me, they wouldn't help me" you might even think "They'd love that, they'll laugh at me". *I doubt that very much.*

If that voice inside of you is telling you that, you need to silence it. Here is how you do it:

Let's work on an apology.

Ouch! That's pretty hard to do too. *I told you at the very beginning of this book that it wasn't going to be an easy book to get through.*

When I talk about an apology I mean a *proper apology*. Not turning up and mumbling "I'm sorry" and giving a really soft handshake for something that happened ages ago – leaving that person thinking *"What was all that about?"*

Ok – from now on we are going to try to live with a greater sense of purpose. You wrote it down.

You didn't promise me — you promised it to yourself.

So when you apologise, there are five things that make it a proper, genuine and powerful apology:

1. I want to apologise to you for [say or write down what it is]
2. I'm sorry because [say why you now realise that what you did was wrong — explain it]
3. I want you to know that I have thought about it a lot, and I've changed since then. I'm not going to put anyone through that in future because I'm going to try to do much better. I expect better things of myself now.
4. I want to make up for it, if I can. I want you to understand that this matters to me.
5. And I want you to forgive me for what I did.

That is hugely powerful. Believe it — you will feel incredibly shy and self-conscious when you say that (or write it down and pass that apology to someone). Somehow though, at the same time, you will feel powerful, courageous and you will feel free and so relieved and happy too.

If the person that you want to help you is someone that you feel you have wronged in the past – start by offering them *a genuine apology* – tell them that you haven't forgotten what happened, and that actually you have a sense of feeling ashamed because of it, you thought that they might not help you as a result.

Communicating on this level is a really supercharged experience.

Both you and the other person will find it to be incredibly different and very connecting. It's best to have these conversations one to one.

If that person is a bit stunned – *and quite frankly most people would be by something as strong and powerful and mature as that* – they might need a minute to absorb it and to understand it properly. They probably aren't expecting it at all. You need to understand that they're just human too and they might need a moment to adjust.

The moment will feel like a long time – and if that person is someone that you respect an awful lot – you might feel your heart beating, you might think you're shaking (you might feel that way, and actually you're not).

If you find the strength and the courage to reach out like this you will never forget this moment in your whole life. That person will never forget this moment in their whole life either – and you'll just have to believe me – *that person will come to your assistance with everything that they have.*

The role that they have to play in getting your life back to what you want it to be is all about removing that thing that you identified as the biggest obstacle to your success.

That might be helping you to cope with a drug dependency problem.

It might be helping you because you know that you've been running drugs and getting into County Lines.

It might be that someone very negative is making you do things that you don't want to do any more – and you need that person to leave you alone.

I think, you will know what that thing is for yourself – and you'll need to find the words to explain that. You don't have to take that mentor into all of your ambitions and your positive goals (if you don't want to) – but you've reached out to them because you need someone else to help you to handle this part of the plan at least.

Remember when we talked about 'subjective' versus 'objective' help? Trying to do it all on your own is 'subjective'. Reaching out to this person is about getting objective help — it is stronger, more powerful and it is far more likely to succeed.

You do need to be honest with this person though and sometimes they will tell you things that you might not want to hear. Don't expect that you will always agree with a mentor.

A mentor is an advisor or a guide who will give you the best of their knowledge and experience. It won't always be soft and easy to listen to — sometimes it will be tough. You have to find the strength to respect the fact that they are being honest with you though, and they clearly care about you. It is much, much easier to tell you what you want to hear, right?

Someone who is willing to argue with you — in the most constructive way — without offering you personal insults or abuse, without threatening you, without bullying you — because they want you to do the right thing, is someone very valuable in your life indeed.

It is so much easier to close the door on people like that and turn around and listen to people who will whisper whatever you want to hear, because it gets you to behave in the way that they want you to behave.

Sometimes having a mentor in your life is hard — you have to have the strength to say thank you when they tell you something that is difficult to listen to.

The most intelligent, powerful people in the world try to surround themselves with people who are wise enough and brave enough to tell them what they don't want to hear. These people are difficult to find and historically leaders and powerful men and women are criticised because they surround themselves with 'yes men' – people that just agree with whatever it is that they have to say.

When it comes to the most difficult times, the 'yes men' melt away in your life. They are never there to take responsibility for their bad advice, they don't stand by you when it gets hard or tough.

A proper mentor is still in your corner when you are at your lowest, reminding you that they believe in you and they you are on the same team and you can both do much better (and that you will do much better). We all need that in our lives. We are actually really lucky if we can count a handful of people in that bracket at any one time or in our whole lifetime.

There will be plenty of people who will tell us that everything is fine and talk to us about what we want to hear. You need to beware of false friends though. *When someone treats you like you're a disposal part of their life – you shouldn't be taking advice from them on subjects that your life or future might depend upon.*

You might also have to accept that a good mentor won't act like your friend. They're giving you good advice, they're looking out for you, they pointing you in the right direction, they never give up on you – but they don't buy you cards on your birthday, they don't want to hang-out with you or play computer games, they won't let you call them by a nick name. A mentor is generally someone that you respect and look up to – so you need to reward them by showing them that respect.

If they give you some advice – and they've taken the time to think about your situation from your point of view – the least you can do is try that advice out. If you sit down every week for one hour with that mentor, and they ask you "Did you try what I suggested?" – and all you ever say is "No" or "I forgot to" (because actually it was uncomfortable, or you didn't want to try it), that's actually a bit insulting and dismissive. Be careful not to give your mentor that impression!

When you come back to them and you have tried the things that they have suggested – for example they advise you to read a book, or watch a specific film, or to create a list of your thoughts about something – make it important that you do those things. That will strengthen your relationship and you will gain strength and knowledge from doing it.

If your mentor feels like you're not listening, not paying attention, and that you don't take things on board – eventually they'll stop supporting you, or they'll tell you very honestly about how it makes them feel.

It's very insincere to go to someone and ask them for advice – but to disregard the advice just because it wasn't the advice you were hoping they would give.

One thing that I have seen many, many times is the person who keeps asking people for advice until they find the person who gives them the advice they were looking for in the first place!

When I was in the police this was commonly one of the most junior Constables. As a Sergeant they'd come to you for advice "How should I deal with this situation?". You would patiently explain what you thought the best course of action was.

Perhaps an hour of two later you would find that Constable doing almost entirely the opposite thing to what you advised. You then find that before they asked you they had asked several other people – and after you they asked several more. Eventually they encountered someone who told them what they wanted to hear in the first place – *and now they were doing that.*

Imagine – the next time that Constable comes to you for advice, are you going to spend a long time with them?

In order to improve your life and get it back to the place where you want it to be, the chances are that you will need to listen to some advice that you don't want to hear. You'll have to take a deep breath, and not just listen to that advice – but you'll have to be brave enough, and courageous enough to actually take that advice too.

Having been this positive – and this strong – to get to this point in this quite challenging book, you might be thinking "Fine – but how do I choose the person that I should go to?"

That's why the next chapter is called ***"Who can I turn to for help or advice?"***

Chapter 5: Who can I turn to for help or advice?

When you're in a difficult position – or you need answers to difficult questions – it is absolutely crucial that you turn to the right person or people for answers. That's really what this chapter is all about – helping you to identify the people who are going to be there to help you.

What is just as important is knowing who not to go to for answers – so we will look at that too.

Here's some of the people that you can turn to for help – and I'm going to divide this down between the people that you can speak to confidentially, and the people that you have to expect to do something about the things you tell them.

What's definitely important to understand is that where a professional can't promise you that they can be confidential (keep a secret) they will only be sharing information to protect you and other people. The way that they share information should be done in a way that reassures you – so that you know what is going to happen next and that there are no surprises. They have a responsibility to protect you. You should talk to them about what happens next and be honest about any anxieties or worries that you have about asking for help. The important thing is that you are communicating. The thing that makes you most vulnerable and at risk of bad things happening is being isolated from people you can genuinely trust and the people who really want to help and support you.

The type of advice and guidance that is available here is not just for the most difficult and severe cases. **This chapter is here to help anyone who feels the need to seek help or answer on any questions at all.**

Parents

Ok, so let's start at the top of the list. Mum or Dad can be a really great choice as someone you can turn to – although I appreciate that is not always easy.

Sometimes people have very difficult relationships with Mum or Dad – and your parents might not live together anymore – which can create more tension depending on whether they are speaking to each other and how they get along.

The whole situation can be very tricky. Also, Mum or Dad do tend to be emotionally invested in you. By that I mean that what you say has an emotional effect on them — if you turn around to Mum or Dad and say (for example)

"I've got a real problem because I started smoking weed this Summer and I owe this guy a lot of money and he has started asking me to do things..."

Depending on how your Mum or Dad is with you — what their character is like, their mood, and what they are going through at the moment — that could be quite an explosive revelation. This makes it hard for you to have the kind of relationship where they are really calm, or they give you advice that you don't like but you are able to accept it in a mature way and so on.

I'm not saying that you don't go to your Mum and Dad with this type of thing — but you can expect certain reactions and outcomes, and it probably will be emotionally charged. Sometimes it helps if you find the right person to confide in who can help you to talk to your Mum or Dad and reassure them that you're ok, but you are going to need a bit of help.

Mums and Dads are people too. It's hard to be a parent — and you might have children of your own one day. You'll suddenly realise that this baby that you've been given didn't arrive with any instructions. You get very little guidance or support on how to be a fantastic parent, and there is an awful lot of pressure to try to get it right.

Naturally, Mum and Dad will usually feel a really strong sense of responsibility and an emotional bond with their child — but not all parents demonstrate that in the clearest way. Being human means that we all make mistakes and we all have our strengths and weaknesses.

If your Mum or Dad is a person who is easily alarmed by these types of problems, has difficult expressing their emotions or tends to react before they really think it through — you might benefit from having someone supporting you when you tell them about what you are going through.

If your Mum or Dad are really calm, and generally show you that you can tell them anything — you're lucky, very lucky. Don't take that for granted — but they are clearly someone you can reach out to. In either regard, you should have a plan about how you are going to explain things to them.

Teachers & Pastoral Care Leads at School

Most teachers are quite misunderstood in a lot of ways. It's a very busy job with a lot of pressure. The sheer time management of running classes and delivering lessons is a big challenge – and let's face it, a lot of teachers get an unfair amount of rude treatment from the young people that they teach.

In reality, teachers go into the profession of teaching because educating and helping people to learn and grow is important to them. They are passionate about their subject and they genuinely want to make a difference in the lives of young people.

At the same time – as professionals - they are emotionally detached and removed enough to give you advice – without feeling threatened by your vulnerability and the risk that is surrounding you.

Teachers make excellent mentors – if you can find the teacher that you have a particular bond with. You do need that rapport – but in my experience everyone has a favourite teacher at school. I've yet to meet anyone, no matter what their situation is, who hasn't met a teacher that they actually like and get along with.

[Mr Kirkham and Mr Cox, if you ever read this thank you for all you did for me]

Pastoral Care Leaders are generally people who work in schools and they are devoted only to the issues of protecting children and young people. They work in teams that look at emotional needs, and they address the things that influence your feelings of wellbeing and security.

As a result Pastoral Leaders are often very approachable – they are not as preoccupied with your grades, or your homework, and they are set back slightly from many of the behavioural issues that might be troubling you. Pastoral Leaders do tend to invest time in learning about subjects like County Lines, Child Criminal Exploitation and Child Sexual Exploitation – all the relevant topics that help them to be able to answer the questions you might have. Some Pastoral Leaders are trained in additional mentoring skills, in counselling, and other ways that can help you (such as delivering Mindfulness skills or guided meditation – if you're willing to give it a try!).

Schools are usually structured in a way to give additional support and guidance – and you simply might not have met the person that can give you the most support and the type of reassurance that you need yet.

Importantly teachers and Pastoral Leaders are DBS checked (Disclosure and Barring Services). This means that their background is clean and free of criminality, which is really important, because you can rely on their integrity and the fact that they are not going to try to manipulate you or steer you into something negative or illegal.

Teachers and Pastoral Leaders do have to make a record of the fact that you have approached them with a problem or an issue – and what that concern was.

Social Workers and YPWs

Social Workers and Young Peoples' Workers come from a background that is not based in your school. They can come into your school to give you extra support and help – but they are not employed by your school, they are generally employed by the County Council through Social Care services or paid for through a local charity on a not for profit basis.

Access to a Social Worker or a YPW has usually been organised following concerns for your welfare or because someone has already identified that you would benefit from additional support or help.

Sometimes YPWs have drop-in clinics at schools and in other places that young people go to commonly – open door sessions where you can find out about the types of help that they can offer. These types of sessions help you to get to know them, and find out if you warm to them. As I think we've already said – being able to have that type of regard for someone really helps the process of opening up and talking about your worries.

All Social Workers and YPWs have to be background checked too – so again you can trust the fact that they don't have a criminal history.

Social Workers and YPWs also have to make a record of the fact that you've talked and the nature of what you discussed. If the nature of what you discussed includes a confession, or a statement of particular concern they are likely to share that with your school and/or parents – but they'll do that in a professional and supportive way.

Doctors & Nurses

Your General Practitioner (G.P.) is a good person to speak to if you have worries about your health or mental or emotional wellbeing. They can refer you to CASUS (Child & Adolescent Substance Misuse Service) or CAMHS (Child & Adolescent

Mental Health Services) where, if necessary, you can speak to a subject matter expert.

This is really important if you're struggling with a problem around using drugs – whether that is weed or anything else.

G.P.s are very busy people and it can be quite intimidating sitting in front of a very busy doctor and just telling them what's on your mind. If it's just advice and guidance that you need I can think of better people to steer you towards, but if you've been smoking weed (for example) and you're starting to see signs or symptoms of psychosis, anxiety or depression I would definitely recommend talking to your doctor.

Most G.P.s practices have community nurses that are great for a wide range of concerns and issues. They tend to be less pressured for time and can find more opportunities to speak to you at length, and really listen to your worries. If you're not sure that you need to talk to the doctor, seeing the community nurse can be a good idea as they'll help you to know whether a doctor's appointment is needed. They can also make referrals to other services like CAMHS and CASUS.

Talking to your doctor has a measure of confidentiality – but if you're not 18 you may have to have a parent with you or another appropriate adult, and the doctor may be obliged to update your parents on the fact that you've had a consultation and what that consultation was about.

Specialist Services

We have talked about two specialist services – CAMHS and CASUS. The people who work in CAMHS will overlap with the people in CASUS – their skills and expertise are usually interchangeable.

We are talking about professional mental health nurses, psychiatrists (specialist doctors that deal with the function of the brain and your mental health), qualified counsellors and people who have an intimate knowledge of how best to deal with issues of either drug or substance misuse, or depression, anxiety, and other signs and symptoms of poor mental health.

Be reassured that we all have mental health – and just like physical health we have periods in our life where our health is good, and times in our life when our health is poor. People used to look at other people struggling with mental health problems as being unusual or 'broken' or even 'mad' – but we're now starting to understand that we can do lots of things to improve our mental health and to help us to cope and feel happier and more confident. There is nothing wrong with identifying that you are struggling and need help and support – in fact this is all part and parcel of an effective measure of self-knowledge and understanding. If you get to a place where you can recognise that you need to ask for help – and you find the courage to ask for it – that is a really positive thing.

Specialist services like CAMHS and CASUS can be referred to from a lot of different places – and very often you can visit their website and you can even self-refer.

These people are all professionals who have a wealth of personal knowledge, experience and training – we don't generally have enough of these people so time with them is very valuable. Getting to consult with such teams is a massive benefit and you'll get the best possible advice and guidance. They are all background checked and certified.

Religious Leaders

When people are thinking and feeling deeply about things that are making a massive change to their lives they might consult with religious leaders in their community.

If you are from a religious background, and you have been drawn into County Lines or criminal exploitation you might feel that you have let your faith down.

I grew up on the Catholic Church – but most religious faiths and denominations afford opportunities for members of the parish or congregation to speak to their Priest, their Imam, Rabbi or otherwise to take guidance on a confidential basis.

If your religion is very important to you – and part of the internal conflict that you have been feeling comes from a place where you feel that you are not upholding your faith the way that you should be – this conversation might be an essential one.

You will need to speak to your pastor or your congregational leader to find out whether your faith or denomination provides that type of counselling and support, and how confidential such support is.

Most religious congregations are supportive environments – but they may judge you for the choices and the decisions that you have made.

As with speaking to your parents, making a 'confession' or a disclosure to your Priest, Rabbi or Imam might be a more emotionally charged experience, and it might be helped by bringing someone to support you and explain the circumstances that you are in.

The strength of knowledge that they have on this subject will vary depending on who you are speaking to.

Whereas a subject of this nature is key to the role that all of the other professionals I have mentioned take – there is nothing necessarily to guarantee that any of our religious communities are particularly trained in this area (though they may be).

Most religious communities do encourage a sense of self- awareness and the development of sympathy, empathy and compassion – which is a positive and constructive thing in helping you to address your worries and concerns.

Talk to Frank and online services

There are pros and cons to online interactive advice. On the plus side most of the services are anonymous – and if you're worried about venturing into giving a full account of your problem, worry or concern out to someone – this type of environment can be a place when you get an initial amount of knowledge and understanding first.

I mention Talk to Frank particularly because it's a very good example of anonymous online help. Every day between 2PM and 6PM there are online drug counselling sessions on a one to one basis. The sessions are free, you don't need an appointment, and you don't have to give your name or identify yourself. These sessions last as long as you want them to or until all of your questions have been answered. At the end they often send you a link to an information page that is relevant to what you've been talking about.

You can expect 'Talk to Frank' to treat you like a grown-up, they don't judge you or look down on you at all. They also have pages of information written by young people who have got involved with different drugs – and they talk in a balanced way about what it was that they enjoyed, what drew them in, and what worried them or wasn't good about doing that drug. There are young people who have said that they do use weed and they want to keep using weed. There are others who have used it, whose use has escalated, and they have gone looking for the help they need to stop using. In this way 'Talk to Frank' is a good, well rounded service that doesn't try to suggest that it's all about 'just say no' and blaming everything on 'peer pressure'.

The downside to 'Talk to Frank' and other anonymous websites is that, actually, they can feel a bit impersonal. You don't get the warmth or rapport or reassurance that you get from speaking to someone you trust or look up to. If you have anxiety that – *for example* – you've been smoking weed and you're starting to suffer with depression or anxiety, it's not easy to feel reassured by someone typing a message back to you that tells you *"Yes, those are symptoms that can be associated with use of cannabis you might want to think about seeing a doctor"*. The level of emotional engagement is quite low.

As a first step I would say that using a service like this is a good thing – it can help you to build up your knowledge and understanding. You might be really worried about something that you don't need to be worried about – and they could help to reassure you about that straight away. Additionally, it could help to encourage you to seek out the right person on a face to face basis – because you feel less foolish and that you know what you're talking about.

As a long term way to deal with a substantial worry that has come out of using drugs, or getting involved in County Lines or criminal exploitation (and Talk to Frank is not really a resource that is tailored to the latter two issues) – *you're probably going to need more help than you'll find there.* Speaking face to face to a trained professional who can give you undivided attention is something that is difficult to improve on.

Anything that can help you to identify the best form of long term advice and support can only be a good thing. Also, services like 'Talk to Frank' can really help on some myth busting – so if someone tells you 'nothing bad ever happens to people who do...' – you can expect 'Talk to Frank' to give you an honest view on the ups and downs of any particular substance.

At the end of this book I'm going to list some websites that I think are really good at giving help and advice – sites that you might want to visit as you find out more about these topics.

As with the other sources of advice and support that we've talked about, the resources I'm going to give you are reliable, have been verified independently, and they are giving our guidance that is backed by experience, professionalism and research.

We can all find a less reputable source of advice or support on anything via the web. If you're a member of a football forum and the people are in there talking about transfer rumours – and you get talking privately to someone about weed, or pills, or coke – you generally have no idea who you are talking to, what their levels of knowledge are, where their bias comes from. It's no better than walking into a pub, or a fast-food restaurant, or a supermarket, finding the first person you encounter, and asking them for an opinion.

What sort of advice should I avoid?

Well in the most simple and straightforward way you should always ask yourself "What gives this person the right to advise me?"

As I write this book for you now, I draw on the experiences that I've had in years of policing, of working in education, on sitting down with professionals in many fields of child protection, and countless times that I worked with parents. I'm drawing on problem solving qualifications and experiences in a relevant area.

Being able to give you advice and guidance in this area would not make me a person to come to if you needed a wisdom tooth extracted, you needed electrical work done at home or you wondered if next season flared trousers were going to be fashionable again. *I'm a genuinely terrible dentist, a very questionable electrician and my fashion sense is slightly more painful than my dentistry.*

The fact is that, if you did have a wisdom tooth problem, a cavity or a broken tooth you absolutely would go to a dentist. If you broke your leg you'd be quite dismayed if an ambulance turned up and then took you to a Chinese takeaway.

So operate with the level of certainty that you're getting your advice and support from someone who can actually advise and support you.

Here are some of the examples that you ought to look out for and avoid:

Friends or people in your friendship group

Now, generally, a good friend gives good advice – but I would suggest that someone in your peer group is likely to be as well informed or (alternatively) lacking in information as you are – more or less. They might be good for emotional support, encouraging you to speak to an appropriate expert – *but it can also go very wrong*.

If they are also experimenting and you know them because they've kind of been drawn into the things that you have been – they're more likely to say that everything is fine and that you don't need to change. We call this 'co-dependency' – where two people who are going through a cycle of drug misuse enable each other to keep doing it by reassuring each other that it's ok. Perhaps they buy it together and split the cost and doing other things to normalise what is happening.

The person who supplies you

If it is a drug misuse issue that you're worried about the last thing to do it ask your dealer for advice. His advice (one way or another) will be "Nah, it's fine, you're good, keep buying". They may see it as an opportunity to transition you to buying other things. "Oh you feel less alert because you're smoking weed? Yeah I get that too – that's why I take a little bit of this in the morning..." (pointing you in the direction of a stimulant like amphetamines).

They are not going turn around and give you that 'objective' advice that we have been talking about. They are not going to put your interests in front of your own. They are motivated by money and the need to keep you buying. It doesn't matter how long you have known this person – the fact that they introduced you to, or sustained you on drugs in the first place is not a good sign.

Strangers and random people on the internet

If you want to you can find a website out that will promote anything. The internet is a wonderful thing, but one downside is that anyone can publish anything on the web – they just need the very small cost to buy the domain and host the website. Websites can be uploaded and hosted from mobile phones and tablets these days – and while it used to be the case that simply looking at the quality of the website told you everything you needed to know about the people behind it – these days it is very easy to make a solid and quite convincing website.

I could sign post you to websites that want you to believe that the Queen is actually an intergalactic Lizard person (genuinely), that the earth is completely flat, or that the moon landings were filmed in a basement in California.

I encourage people frequently to test what they read before they accept it as truth. If you want to know how trustworthy a source is, type the name of the website into your preferred search engine with the word 'scam', 'fake' or 'reliable?' – any reports about that website will come up and you might be surprised by what you read there.

You might think something is reliable because it has been hosted on a website that you like or think it is genuine. Facebook recently created a real argument in the US when it refused to verify what advertisers published – **even if they know something to be false, they will accept the advertising money and publish the advertisement anyway.**

The vast majority of information that comes through to us is delivered in headlines and soundbites, media quotes and one-liners. Before you know it, you've read it, you haven't had time to check it and you end up believing it because people repeat it.

You need to be savvy online and you need to challenge what you read and what you trust. Use verified sources, people with credentials, and search up on the background of the person that you're reading to see how much trust other people have in what that source is saying.

All of the sources and people that I've recommended have been verified, have been subject to background checks, they are independent, and *most importantly* – they care about you as an individual – not about something else (like their profits, their drugs or the fact that they are doing certain things themselves).

Chapter Six: How do I help my friend?

Helping a friend can be tricky. Not all of your friends want to be helped – even if they need help, *and you know that they do need help*. A person who doesn't want help cannot be helped. As the saying goes –

> **"You can take a horse to water, but you can't make it drink"**

This is really hard.

Let's consider both of the situations – where you have a friend who has come to you for help, and the more difficult situation where you have a friend who you think does need help, but actually they are not receptive to it and don't welcome it.

We'll start by looking at signs and symptoms. These are the things that – if you see them in a good friend – it should be a clear warning that it might be time for you to talk to them, or to bring it to the attention of someone else who can talk to them supportively:

Signs and symptoms

You've got a friend, you've known them for a long time, but all of a sudden, they've changed:

- They have new fancy designer possessions and you can't really explain where they've come from (mobile phone, trainers, clothing…);
- They start changing their mobile phone frequently or you know that they are carrying more than one mobile phone;
- They've changed their friendship group and you're seeing less of them. They're getting distant and you don't know the people they are moving towards *or* the people they are moving towards are definitely into drink/drugs;
- They've become angry, hostile, confrontational and their moods seem irrational and difficult to explain;
- They're suddenly not coming into school regularly and they're missing lessons too;
- They've started going missing from home – maybe their mum and dad have asked you if they know where they've been going?
- They're no longer interested in things that they used to be – abandon the

- football team, gymnastics, music or clubs and societies unexpectedly;
- They start talking about making trips into London or to another big city alone – maybe ask you to come along;
- You know that they've started experimenting with drugs and they're talking to you about it;
- They want you to start doing drugs or joining them in risk taking behaviours that you're uncomfortable with;
- They are selling drugs to friends or other people in or outside of school;
- You know they've started carrying a weapon habitually and they seem paranoid or have even threatened you;

If you see these things happening to a friend you are right to be worried. You might be concerned about 'snitching' – but honestly, I'm asking you to do something that is really important and that in the years to come they will be grateful to you for.

A really important thing to be aware of though, is that as a good friend – using those qualities of sympathy, empathy and compassion – sometimes we have to put the friend in front of the friendship, and risk making them unhappy or angry in the short term.

You might find that, having recognised several of those matters that give you concern, that your friend is actually quite hostile if you approach them and ask them what is going on. They could respond angrily *"Are you actually accusing me...?"* they might try to laugh it off *"You're joking don't be ridiculous"* or they might even try to ridicule you *"Who do you think you are?"*. If your friend is hostile to your help – and/or you are not satisfied by their response (for example they give you a very weak explanation) – you have to back away. Don't get drawn into an argument. Being 'right' won't help here.

It's important that you pick a good place and a good time to address something like this. You don't drop something like this onto someone *"Oh by the way, I've been thinking about it and I'm worried that you've become a drug dealer"*. Try to do it in a setting where you're not rushed, try to do it somewhere that is private, you need to do it face to face and not over social media DMs, and you need to be able to put a lot of emphasis on the fact that you are doing this because you care about them.

You really need to know this person extremely well (or think you do). Don't approach someone you *half know*, or know through someone, this is strictly best friend/close friend territory. If you recognise these qualities in someone else, you need to go to a trusted adult and hand these concerns over to them.

Understand the limitation of your skills and abilities

Just because you don't provide all the solutions to the problems, it doesn't mean that you haven't helped massively. You are not expected to be a drug counsellor, or someone who can extract someone from County Lines. There are experts in this subject who find this work incredibly difficult after years of experience.

You have to know when to draw a line and step back. If you go to a friend and you offer them your support and concern – and they refuse it – you also have to look after your own welfare. Make a decision – are you going to go and speak to an adult professional (I would strongly recommend this course of action, but it is your choice)? If you are – *go and do it* – if you're not, then you need to be able to reconcile yourself to the fact that you're going to distance yourself from the problems your friend is having and watch what is unfolding from a safe distance. **For goodness sake, do not follow them into a burning building though!**

It's rare in this book that I'm going to try to tell you exactly what to do – but I feel that I need to right now:

Think about a situation that is a catastrophe – a terrible accident of some sort. A burning building, a sinking ship – you and your friend are in that situation. You're able to get out, and you're able to get your friend out too – if they will let you. If they won't follow you, or get out to save themselves, **you must not stay there and suffer the same outcome.**

Even if your friend is very receptive to the efforts that you are making to help them – you have to know that you have human limits in what you can do. We all do. Be honest with yourself about what your limits are in terms of your age, your time, your knowledge, and the things that you can change around someone else. Sometimes the most helpful thing to do is to encourage someone to sit down with another person that can bring additional expertise and experience to the situation.

We've talked about self-knowledge being really important. This is one of the situations where knowing yourself becomes critically (very, very) important. One of the worst things in the world is giving advice to someone that you think is good advice – and seeing that well intentioned advice go badly and lead to a negative outcome. *It is a lot of responsibility to take.*

So be honest with yourself about that – and be honest with your friend too. Having a conversation where you say to your friend:

> *"You are a really good friend to me and I care about you an awful lot – I don't know about this very much more than you do – if I give you the wrong advice I don't think I'll be able to cope with that very well. I want us to speak to someone…"*

The fact is that when someone gets involved in drugs, County Lines, in criminal exploitation – this is very high risk stuff.

People who get involved in these issues can get very badly hurt. You do not want to put yourself into a position where you become part of what we call 'the chain of causation'.

A 'chain of causation' scenario is one where the actions that you took – the advice that you gave – was so influential and key that, without your involvement, something else wouldn't have happened which then led directly to a particularly bad outcome.

When people get into these situations we do end up facing outcomes that include self-harm, suicide, accidental overdoses, being robbed, assaulted or subject to sexual assaults. As I'm writing this book I want you to be thoughtful about the fact that you shouldn't put yourself in a position where emotionally and psychologically you are scarred by the best efforts you have taken to protect or help a very good friend.

That is why going and finding an adult professional that you trust and respect very much, is absolutely essential.

Thinking things through

Sitting down with a trusted adult is the most important next step. You cannot (you really shouldn't), in this situation, act as a secret keeper. So decide who *you* are going to confide in – and choose that person well.

You're going to sit down and talk your concerns through. So prepare yourself in a proper way – be methodical and get it in order. It might help you to write this stuff down.

Before you talk to this person – ask yourself these key questions:

What is the situation?

Who is involved and who are you concerned about?

When did you last know this to be true?

Why do you believe this to be the case?

On a scale of 1 – 10 how certain are you about the things you are fearing?

Is there a prominent risk that worries you particularly?

How immediate do you think the risk is?

How did you get to know about this?

Who else knows?

Who else have you discussed it with?

Has the person that you are confiding about told you anything that has confirmed the fears that you currently have?

Has the person that you are confiding about given you any indication that they are looking for help or feel that they are in immediate danger?

Does that person know you are seeking help?

How do you feel about your name being connected to this information or would you prefer to remain anonymous?

There is a possibility that if your friend won't do what they really ought to do — *and if they are planning to do something really dangerous* — that someone in authority will have to intervene.

Look at the type situation — *let's say you are a girl aged 14 and your friend in the same year at school says that she has been asked to go to a party with a boy. The boy is 17 and the party is in Birmingham. The boy left school last year and was known for being involved in drugs. Your friend wants to tell her mum that she is staying at your house, and for you to cover for her so that she can go to the party and stay there overnight with this boy. She really likes this boy and she believes that they've fallen in love. She has told you that she has decided that at the party she is going to have sex for the first time.*

[This is not a particularly creative piece of writing for me to offer because it's surprisingly common.]

In that situation there is a very real possibility that the 17 year old boy has been told by someone else to bring young girls to a specific party in Birmingham (more than 50 miles away). The use of drugs is highly likely and the purpose of that drug use is not just for fun — but by men who want to make it harder for girls to say no to them. There is a very real possibility that your friend is about to be trafficked as part of a larger plan to supply drugs and sex – and she could be raped or sexually abused at that 'party' if you 'cover for her'.

On the other side of that situation, if you *do* cover for her, it will come out that you played a part in that happening. Put yourself in a position a day later, where you discover that a friend was groomed and sexually abused – you saw and recognised what was happening – but you didn't intervene. *Did you become part of a chain of causation?*

Of course her Mum will say "I thought she was staying with _____" [insert your name]. You can basically either lie to the police and say that you didn't know anything about it, or try to persuade them that you didn't think she was in danger so you went along with it.

You won't be in trouble with the law – you didn't do something that intentionally supported a human trafficking offence – *but will you ever be able to live with yourself knowing that you could have put a stop to it?*

In this situation – yes – the police might have to intervene before your friend makes that mistake. In likelihood, your teachers or someone else could intervene to stop that journey. Regardless of who it is – it's a difficult decision to make – but

I know who I think is being a better friend, and this being said, it is for you to make up your own mind.

Being strong is an essential part of doing the right thing. If you recognise the signs and the symptoms, and you ask for professional help, you are not over-reacting – you're doing something that could save a life.

Understand how important your contribution is

A good friend in this situation is not there to judge a poor decision or whether they have done right or done wrong. The 'best friend situation' is to help that friend to find their way to safety.

If your friend wants to find help and support they probably need some courage to do the difficult thing that they know they need to do.

Very often they need someone who can be totally honest with them, but in a compassionate way. You need to show them that you care, that you are worried, and that they matter. At times in our lives we all look for guidance and familiarity – someone who can take us by the hand and lead us to the place we know we ought to go. Yes, we know that we should do that thing – but you need someone to help you get there.

You're not expected to be an expert in all things drugs or criminal exploitation related. In fact, I would encourage you to be really honest about that. *"I'm not expert on this, I'm just worried about you"* or *"I don't know a massive amount about this stuff – but I just want to help you"*.

Having someone who can perform that role is absolutely just as important as having someone who knows a lot about cannabis, or crime, or gangs. Everybody needs that person when they are coming back from a really terrible experience – and being able to be that person for someone else is just priceless. I can find a large number of people who have strong qualifications as drug counsellors, who know about crime and gangs, who can explain what is happening when a young person takes drugs – but your friendship is unique. So don't for one minute think that I'm limiting your contribution here – because without that piece of critical support at that time, and probably going forward, I'm pretty sure that we can't get that person the help and support that they need.

How people respond to grief and trauma

There is a very well established pattern that people go through when they are coping with grief. It goes like this:

Shock and denial

This is the state where they are first confronted with a situation. Common examples include losing a loved one - but being confronted with the fact that all they want to do is talk about or smoke drugs — *and that they might be addicted* — that can result in the same outcome as well. "You think *I* have a problem?".

Pain and guilt

This is a very private stage — and you must understand there is no time scale for a person to move through the previous stage (it could be weeks or months before they get here — even years). It might need something specific to happen before they move to this stage. They might go into and through this stage alone, alternatively they might think that they need someone to talk to. *You can't force this* — you can't push a person into the next stage of this cycle, and when they eventually do get there, you can't make them go through it *with you*. This stage might involve them recollecting a shameful event that they were involved in that ultimately only happened to support their use of a drug. For example – if they bullied a smaller younger child to give them money so they could buy weed. If they stole from a parent or loved one, or if they encouraged someone who was vulnerable to use too.

Anger and bargaining

This is a stage where they start to come to terms with the situation. They might not bargain with you – but you are likely to see the anger. *"What's it got to do with you anyway?"*. Remember this is not in direct response to you challenging them (shock and denial) – at that moment you can expect them to offer anger, but it doesn't mean they've got to *this* stage. This stage comes after they actually confront a sense of guilt and they are beginning to admit that there is a problem. What this stage is about is – for example – if they were to say (having come through a great deal of pain and guilt) *"I don't have to sell weed to smoke weed. I could just smoke less weed – I just got a bit carried away. I can just smoke a bit of weed, pay for it like everyone else, and I just won't do it around you – what's so bad about that?"*

The trouble is that people who go into anger and bargaining over drug misuse usually *know* that they're in too deep. They're only really trying to bargain with themselves — they are making suggestions that they know they can't keep to and the anger they have is anger at themselves more than anyone else. Despite this, it is anger that can be projected in very real ways towards the people they love the most. Anyone who comes between them and the drug that they really want to do can experience a very real back lash and you have to know when to back away from that. *It is not your job to intervene and prevent them from being able to make their own mistakes.* All you can do is say "You have to do what you think you have to do."

You have to know — in yourself - when to draw the line and walk away though. You must always look after your own welfare.

> *"If you want to smoke drugs or take pills we are not going to be friends because I'm just not into that. I'm not judging you — and I'll always care about you — but that's just who I am".*

It's my advice to you that you should never let someone who is using drugs bargain you into a position where you change *your* choices because of the drugs *they* are doing. Protect yourself first and foremost. This is really painful — but it's my honest advice.

Depression

It's actually really common when people have been through an experience with drugs, that if they come out the other side of it and get clean, they may fall into depression. If a person gets into drugs and a drug related lifestyle it's a really powerful thing. They will be broken hearted in a way. There is a reason why so many rock stars have written thinly veiled love songs about cocaine or heroin.

There is a very powerful American film called 'Requiem for a Dream' (18). It was a small, very cool, but very graphic indie film that came out in 2000 that didn't have a massive budget and didn't depend on lots of big special effects. It was made for $4.5 million — which is movie terms is literally regarded as nothing. *The latest Star Wars film cost something like $250 million.*

A 'requiem' is a type of religious ceremony that someone has when someone dies. A requiem is about coping with and acknowledging a death. In this film the whole piece is about 'the dream' and 'the dream' is the idea of finding a drug that is so wonderful that you build your life around it. You sell enough of it to other people that not only can you afford *your* drugs, it also makes you rich and gives you all the material rewards you want in life too, making you very popular along the way.

Getting pulled into County Lines is like that. If you've been sexually exploited you might have convinced yourself you actually were in love with someone. You might have got so into a drug that you think you've found a short cut to who you want to be, and it makes you feel and experience life in a particular way. You trick yourself into thinking you've discovered an alternative state of being. You want to shut yourself away from everything and just have that drug.

The truth is – and the truth that is expressed in 'Requiem for a Dream' - is that drug abuse and dependency always spirals, and generally while you might start off in a position where you can sell enough drugs to pay for your own habit and create other positive financial outcomes – *it's only a matter of time before the drugs take over and your life starts to fall apart*. You physically cannot be selling and supplying drugs if you only want to lay in bed and get high. You only end up owing money to someone for the drugs you are using.

The early stages of love – infatuation and euphoria – are exactly the same and operate in the brain in exactly the same place. When two people meet each other and fall in love (even in the most healthy way), they just want to spend time in each other's company (and this sometimes annoys their friends hugely).

In Arabic literature there are supposed to be seven stages of love: hub (attraction), uns (infatuation), ishq (love), akidat (trust), ibadat (worship), junoon (madness) and maut (death). While we tend to treat *'falling in love'* (usually with someone) as a wholly positive experience – we have to understand that falling in love with the wrong thing is very much like addiction. *Addiction is hugely damaging.* Nobody is ever quite as weak or vulnerable as when they are in a damaging relationship either with a person or something that hurts them.

So in many way, your friend is bound to get much more unhappy as a person, before they round the corner and start to feel happier again. It is unlikely that they will ever go back to being quite the same person you knew before they got involved in all this.

While a very detached and removed person might feel pity for someone in this situation – *we know we can do better than that.* Sympathy understands that this person is in real pain, empathy helps us to understand that we've hurt ourselves making mistakes before and we could even make the same mistake – it could happen to anyone. Compassion helps us to understand and do something for that person (where they allow us to).

Depression is an awful thing to go through – a clinical condition – and nobody needs a friend more than someone who is going through that.

The Upward Turn

A person who goes through the depression stage will eventually, usually, go into a more optimistic stage called 'the upwards turn'. This is a fragile, gentle place where slowly they start to think about small things that make them feel happier. A person with crippling depression might get out of bed for the first time in days or weeks. It is very much like seeing the first green shoots of a plant coming out of the soil in Springtime. Your instinct might be to leap on that and encourage them to do so much more – but as a friend this is just about being there – saying "Well done" in a very calm way, and just going with the pace they have set for themselves.

Reconstruction

This is where they actually start to look at the damage that has been done to their lives and eventually – when they come to terms with that - it leads to acceptance and hope.

Acceptance and hope

Acceptance and hope is the final stage – it is a genuine acknowledgement of the problem in the most objective way, without bargaining or anger, and having come through depression. People talk about feeling 'centred' – which is an emotional place of stability that is not happy or sad. They see 'what it is' for 'what it is', and they realise that they are still alive and that there is a future ahead.

What is critically important – *absolutely the most important thing in all this* – is that you understand that your friend cannot be helped through all this by you on your own. You are not emotionally equipped to carry anyone through all this – particularly without telling other people or by trying to keep it a secret.

This isn't about you having shortcomings or me saying 'you're not up to it'. I'm not saying this because you're a young person and because I'm an adult. I don't have the emotional strength to carry a person through all this alone. I don't think that anyone does.

Success through all this is about having different people who play different roles to support the things that your friend needs. You have a very significant role to play in supporting your friend – but please do not try to do this all on your own.

Chapter Seven: Looking forward to better things

The threat of County Lines, drug abuse and dependency, criminal exploitation or child sexual exploitation is very much about the threat that is posed to your ability to see a better future for yourself.

I accept and I understand that as a reader you might have come to this book from any kind of a background, and with any level of advantage or disadvantage.

You might have picked it up in a library, you might have been given a copy to read by school – a concerned friend might have bought it for you.

I really do appreciate that your way of life might make you feel quite trapped sometimes. You might not have access to luxury things or material possessions that you would like to have around you. Your trainers and clothes might not be as 'designer' as other people in your school. You might feel insecure and you might think that you'd be more popular if you did have those things.

County Lines is really about feeding on your fear. Your fear that there is no other way that you're ever going to get your chance to enjoy those things – the things that everyone else seems to have plenty of.

A shortcut is incredibly tempting – but in County Lines everything leads to something else. It's about drawing you into something really negative, and ultimately gaining control over the choices that you can make in your life.

One of the most powerful things that you have is your freedom of choice. Your ability to choose your future is particularly important here.

If you want to have a future that is financially well rewarded you can – absolutely – go out and claim that for yourself. There are lots of legitimate careers where if you get the right qualifications you can expect to be financially very well rewarded for the time you invest in learning and passing those exams or gaining those skills.

This is money that you don't have to hide, that you can spend as you wish, and that means you don't have to look over your shoulder for the rest of your life. You don't have to expect the police to knock on your front door, or be worried that people are following you.

In truth County Lines is hard work – not easy money. It's incredibly hard work. Hugely demanding with very little sense of freedom. Your phone goes off and you have to do what you are told. The consequences of not doing as you are total can be brutal and very scary. Inside the world of County Lines there is no fairness, no police, no protection – you are in a desperate position where you are depending on the kindness of people who don't believe in sympathy, empathy or compassion.

Being outside of the County Lines system – being free of it – is about reclaiming your life. It's being allowed to like what you like, be with the people that you love and respect, and choose the things that really make you happy.

Nobody expects you to be wealthy as a teenager. It's not actually normal or average to be able to go and spend £250 on your school shoes. You might not get to go skiing twice a year – very few people actually do – *most people don't go skiing every year*, and plenty have never been. You might want to go skiing – you can build a life for yourself where you do that. I know people who *have* done that – and quite rightly they are proud of themselves and what they have achieved.

It is wonderful to see people achieving their dreams and goals. We love to watch the Olympics and see the finals where people win medals. They only got there because they put in years of commitment, discipline, self-belief and hard work. We celebrate with them because we want to see all that rewarded. The villains that society hates are the people who didn't put that work in – but instead they took a performance enhancing drug, found a short cut – and they cheated. When they get found out, in a single moment they go from being the champion and the hero, to being the cheat. Such people create anger and inspire everyone to reject them and dislike them strongly.

Going out and achieving your goals and dreams is not just about the significant moment of being awarded or earning that thing you went after. Maybe you had a goal to buy and drive a Porsche sports car – and that moment when you go and collect the keys and drive it away is unforgettable – but the thing that really makes it what it is, is the memory of how you worked and saved, and what you did to achieve that.

There are a number of online computer games where you have to build a character and evolve and level up – earn a form of in game currency – develop the game world, the home and gather resources. *There is a really funny thing with these games* – take for example the very popular 'Animal Crossing' series on Nintendo. You take a character you have made and over time you want to make this character wealthier and give them more prosperity.

You can actually go online to somewhere like eBay and buy a massive quantity of the in-*game currency ('Bells') from other gamers who will sell it to you for real money. Usually a small amount like £5 will make your character the equivalent of an in-game billionaire.

Anyone who has done this knows one thing – as soon as the immediate excitement of that dies – you've just ruined your game. You have nothing left to do. The game is pointless. *You're immediately bored*.

For many people who win the lottery – for example – particularly the huge Euro-Millions (or in America state or inter-state) lotteries they discover that their whole reality has been changed. They can buy a Porsche in every colour they like. Suddenly what was once worth so much, is now just not worth anything. They *actually* need counselling to come to terms with all this.

We are all guilty of taking things for granted – there are things in our life that we know could simply be better. A common example – your headphones might not be the latest Bluetooth AirPods or Beats designer brand – but without the ones you have, you can't hear your music at all. If you were in a position where you couldn't have any sound, those headphones would be priceless to you.

Growing up I enjoyed computer games – mostly in the primitive second generation 16-bit era. The consoles cost about £120 (maybe equivalent to £300 today) and the games cost £30 or £40 each for an experience that was very basic. We loved those games though and we wanted them. Today retro-consoles cost about £50 and usually come complete with a whole library of 16-bit games built into them – thirty or more. At the time (1990s) my mind would have been completely blown by the idea - £50!! (like £30 then?). If there was County Lines about at that time they would have been offering young people of my age to trade all my freedoms for what is *today* worth £50 on the high street – *and plenty of young people would have done it.*

Materialism is a very funny thing, and as you get older you look back on the things that you really, really wanted, but somehow never did own – and you feel bemused (puzzled and entertained) looking at why you felt that way. They might look ugly now. The technology seems so inadequate and poor. You think about what you really thought about paying – the sacrifices that you nearly decided to make for that thing. You wanted it *so* much! Today it might be available on eBay for next to nothing because nobody wants that anymore. Every landfill site is littered with mobile phones that used to be 'the latest thing'.

It's a really important quality to be able to interrupt yourself when you feel really tempted by something – and to look into the future and think about how you might look back on it in that way. Allow yourself to look forward to better things and take the pressure off yourself to have something immediately and right now. Not being owned and controlled by your desire to have the latest phone, trainers and clothing is a really strong quality to develop.

Being able to look forward to a better future includes preparing yourself for the important and more meaningful things. Knowing yourself, and in the long term what you want to be, is far more rewarding. You might find out that when you sit and think about it – money isn't actually the most important thing to you at all. You might decide that you'd be much happier on a modest wage doing something you love every single day instead. Plenty of people realise this and make this choice. There are lots of variations on this quote – *I didn't come up with it* – and it gets attributed to lots of different people but basically is goes:

> *"If you do what you love, you'll never work a day in your life"*

Nothing beats the excitement of getting up in the morning knowing that the day ahead includes something that is going to make you feel happy.

Writing books has been such an amazing experience for me – I will happily write on my 'day off'. I try to fit it into whatever time I have, and when I'm tired, I want to have energy so that I can write some more. Having the courage to change my career to work with young people every day was huge – it was actually a really scary thing – but it is something that I have never regretted and it makes me happy every day. I can only encourage you – as you read this – to find the thing that you know will make you happy every day, and find a way to make that the basis of your life.

I know people in academic circles who love what they do, I know people in the police who love what they do, and I know people in trades and professions who love what they do. There is – in fact – a whole world out there and you can set your mind and energy to finding the thing that makes you ridiculously happy.

I found out about a guy who, as a marine biologist, spends a huge amount of his time swimming and diving around coral reefs. He captures evidence of the life as it lives and breathes in those environments – in photographs, video, samples, and his writing – because the world needs someone who does that for a job. He gets paid to do that in places like the Great Barrier Reef in Australia.

I spoke with a lady last week who has an international career in helping people to learn about 'Mindfulness' – a therapeutic approach to relaxation and bringing calm into your life. She has worked all over the world from China to America to Holland, and has a series of best selling books which have been read by hundreds of thousands of people all over the world. Her latest book is being translated into Portuguese so that it can be sold in Brazil. Everything she does is devoted to making people feel happy, calm and relaxed (without drugs!).

The truth is that – free from the pressures of drug dependency and criminal exploitation - you are free to explore a whole world of happier options. You have lots of time to think about and consider what you want, and imagine and plan a brilliant future for yourself.

You'd like to open a beachfront bar on a Caribbean island? People do that. You can do that. Live in the sunshine every day, help people to have wonderful holidays, never wear shoes, never own or even need a coat. Fantastic!

I was talking to a friend's mum and she actually grew up in the Caribbean and she told me that she used to get in trouble for talking in class… to the parrots that used to fly in through the open windows of the classroom! She told me that they had a very open classroom to allow the breeze to blow through it because it was a very hot climate – and the brightly coloured parrots used to fly down and perch in and around the classroom distracting the children. I can't imagine how amazing that must have been. It's a lot different to the school I went to!

There are amazing things happening out in the world – and free from a criminal record, free from crime, free from drugs – you can go out into the world and explore those things. The life that you have ahead of you should be long, healthy and exciting.

Anything that anyone else is doing out in the world can be done – so you can find that person who is doing that amazing thing that excites you and makes you happy – and you find out how they got there. Build your efforts towards that and in due course you will be doing the same thing.

Even if the thing that you are really interested in doesn't really exist right now – *it doesn't mean that it won't or that you cannot invent or play a key role in developing it.*

We've already talked about how Bill Gates and Steve Jobs created a world that they wanted to be part of. That world really didn't exist for them as children and young people – but their vision and their enthusiasm made it happen for all of us. We wouldn't really know what to do today without the inventions that they gave us.

This might seem like a staggering and intimidating thing – but it happens on a smaller scale too. I had a friend at school who wanted a life in football. Although we were both pretty good (by schoolboy standards), and our school team was outstanding, neither of us were good enough to realistically think about becoming professional footballers. He still believed that he could earn a good living in football and when coaching certificates came out I thought they looked like a lightweight and faddy choice. He saw a whole industry. His motivation and hard work carried him through his certificates to 'soccer' training camps in America – to bigger qualifications including a degree from an American University and high levels of accreditation as a coach. He was exploring a whole industry as it was only just beginning – he saw something that most other people didn't see. He's a director level coach at a college in America now and he has a wonderful life – very well paid, he is married and has children and his lifestyle is exceptional.

I am always amazed by what he achieved because at school he didn't seem to pay attention and always wanted to laugh or muck about, make other people laugh. I don't think anyone would point to him and say that he was a guy that was going to make it in the way that he did. When he realised what he wanted though, he got very serious about it. He didn't come from a background that was wealthy or full of advantage – he really is an example of what knowing yourself, and knowing what you want, can actually get you.

There are lots of books about the power of positive thinking and how you can empower yourself to achieve your goals and your dreams. Sometimes you have to expose yourself to more optimism (that is happier and more hopeful ways of thinking) about yourself to allow good things to start happening around you.

Sometimes it is so easy to get drawn into the negative and unhappy experiences in your life that you stop even seeing the good stuff that is already there. There are hundreds of great quotes about the power of positive thinking but one that I really like – and I don't know who wrote this:

"What consumes your mind controls your life."

It is so simple and honest. The truth is that having the power to change your thinking patterns, and the way that you respond to the world around you, changes everything in your life. Even in the most difficult circumstances – and it's the most difficult circumstances that tend to lead us to the most amazing successes and victories.

For the football fans – seeing Liverpool 3-0 down to AC Milan before they won the European Cup 4-3 in Istanbul – is evidence that anything really is possible.

The people that we really admire are the ones who just never give up and no matter what won't be denied. They keep going – time and again – to get the things that they have decided are possible and that they want. In that football match it was Steven Gerrard and he made a whole career out of that attitude and it drove him on to higher levels of skill and ability.

Designing the light bulb, Thomas Edison – the most outstanding inventor in the history of

American patent history – made countless version that *didn't* work. He is credited with saying that he knew "100 ways not to make a lightbulb". Of course – in the end – he was proven right. Electricity could be used to create light. Today we depend completely on the fact that he did make this breakthrough.

A man called Roger Bannister decided that it was possible for a human to run a mile in 4 minutes. The world pretty much disagreed and said that this couldn't be done. Bannister did indeed break this boundary – and in doing so, all of a sudden, the world was introduced to a new level of endurance. He opened the door to others and since his achievement in 1954, 1,400 other male athletes have done the same.

In 1932 Amelia Earhart (pronounced 'Air-Heart') became the first woman to fly solo across the Atlantic Ocean. She set records for flying at altitude and went on to fly across the Pacific Ocean solo (the first woman to do so) too. Her incredible achievements were essential to the movement towards global recognition of gender equality and gave huge inspiration to women everywhere that they could achieve great things in a world where women were actively discriminated against.

Part of their achievements were to do with the fact that they could believe in themselves completely – identify and scrub away their sense of personal doubt and fear – and devote themselves to what they thought was really important in their lives. In all three circumstances they actually showed themselves willing to risk their lives to make their achievements and pushed themselves to their very physical and mental limits. In fact Amelia Earhart died in an air disaster in 1937 when she was attempting to fly around the world solo. Her body was never found.

The question of such people giving their lives over to something as short term and empty as drugs or being controlled by someone else for short term material rewards is completely unthinkable. They set their personal value way beyond what anybody could understand and it didn't matter whether other people agreed with it, or understood it. When the other people were preoccupied with saying *why* Roger Bannister couldn't possibly run a mile in under 4 minutes – Bannister was too busy making sure that he could.

Who were these people before they decided to do what they did? Thomas Edison was a telegraph operator in the American Midwest, and he was mostly self-educated. He was deaf and suffered with what is now known as 'attention deficit hyperactivity disorder' or ADHD.

Amelia Earhart was a comparatively well-off girl who grew up with people telling her to be good and trying to push her into things that were expected and acceptable for girls to do ('know her place'). She was financially wiped out by the global economic crisis in the 1920s. She never accepted that there were things that were off limits to her just because she was a woman. *We know that now* – but in her life time it was a whole revolution.

Roger Bannister came from a working class background in the 1920s. He survived his family home being bombed in the 1940s and realised a love of running at school. Despite being from a very modest background he worked hard and succeeded in being accepted to study medicine at Oxford University. In 1947 – at the age of 18 – the best time he could run was a mile in 4.24 (four minutes and twenty four seconds). He was almost half a minute away from running a four minute mile and nobody had ever broken four minutes before. He came fourth in the 1952 Olympics at 1500m – and briefly considered giving up running altogether as a consequence...

All of these people – *who you might never have heard of before* – changed the world around them by having the confidence to invest their time and efforts into the things that really inspired them. They found the things that truly gave them what they were looking for – and despite any disadvantages – they overcame the obstacles to claim their amazing achievements.

You don't have to be one of *these* people to consider yourself a success, either. The point really is this – nobody has the right to tell you that you cannot achieve something. You really can make a difference in the world and to the people around you. You can choose what type of difference that is, and what your success is going to look like.

The success that you achieve defines you. It goes ahead of you and you become known by it – in the same way that negative choices sadly tend to as well. What we are taught by such incredible people is that real achievement and meaningful success comes from long term planning and building towards that success. It might involve an unorthodox or unusual journey to get yourself there. It might involve developing the personal resilience to survive disappointment and setbacks – *in fact it probably will*. It could mean learning how to make sacrifices in the short term to get a much bigger bonus and a much more meaningful reward in the longer term. Most of the people in very successful positions will tell you that you need to strengthen yourself as an individual – build your confidence, surround yourself with positive people, with role models, and people you can genuinely learn from – and not to expect it to come easily. These personal qualities are rare – few people invest enough in themselves to develop them – and that is just one reason why so many people don't fulfil their potential.

Being preoccupied and working hard towards having a good knowledge of yourself will help you to become the type of person that is going to succeed and it will help you to avoid the major mistakes and the painful consequences that are often to be found in County Lines, criminal exploitation, sexual exploitation or drug abuse. There is absolutely no reason for you to have to get drawn into it – and if you have been, there is every reason for you to want to get out.

Postscript

A postscript is a funny thing. This is the part of the book where we sort of round up and reflect on what we've been looking at and boil it down to the most relevant points that I'd really like you to remember and keep with you afterwards.

While this book was always intended to be something that you read in a particular order – from start to finish – I hope it will be something that you can come back to and just read parts of when you want to remember certain things.

We've been on a bit of a journey. I've told you about myself and why I'm writing this book. Remember – I want you to see what I have seen. I've been honest about that and what I have encountered as a result of County Lines – I've given you the truth as I have experienced it over a number of years. I have seen a lot of people who have sunk their lives into false promises and with very damaging consequences.

I'm writing this book – above all else – because I want fewer and fewer people to end up in circles of criminal exploitation and harm.

I know that right now, as I write this, all over Britain there are young people receiving messages and they're getting their bags on and they are going out on the bikes or mopeds to deliver drugs and collect cash.

I know that this weekend – and I'm writing this now on a Saturday – that tonight some girls are going to lie to their parents so that they can go to a party in a strange town or city and see what happens.

Perhaps most upsetting – I know that a lot of the young people I'm writing about – and maybe you are one of them, feel like they have no choice or they have no hope. In the most sympathetic way – if that is you, I want you to read this and know that it is not true – you do have choices.

If you are under 18 and have committed offences while you have been moved from one place to another by someone else – under criminal influence, whether you thought that you consented to do it or not, you have a defence under the Modern Day Slavery Act 2015, for any criminal offences that you committed as a consequence.

This is an acknowledgement from the government and the police that you have been victimised and exploited. You are not the target that the justice system is seeking.

You can go and speak to a person in authority and you can expect to receive protection and compassion from the law.

This is absolutely important for you to understand.

Having read this book – without becoming an expert – you know what County Lines is now. *I certainly don't know everything myself.* So we are on a journey to become better informed together. You may know things that I don't know – speaking up and talking about your experiences might save a life.

You should be able to see now that County Lines is a very cold business model – it doesn't care about you or your friends, and the people who perpetrate crime under the County Lines heading will say or do whatever they have to do in order to use you for their purposes.

They have only one purpose – to make as much money as possible.

They will lie to you. They will bribe you. They will threaten you. They will force you. They will threaten the people that you care about. They will subject you to stalking and harassment. They will gaslight your perceptions of the world. They will pretend that they care about you and love you. They want you, they need you, to believe that what they have is something that you cannot do without (money, drugs, popularity - anything). I hope that by reading this book you can see through to the other side of what they are offering and into what lays behind it all.

We do not want to give power to these people, what they represent, or what they are willing to do.

We have taken the time to look at the different ways in which you might be attracted into and be placed within a world of organised crime.

We have considered how people are identified and groomed. We have looked at how young people and particularly girls in their teens, are exploited sexually. We have considered how someone buying weed can be converted and radicalised to run drugs, sell drugs, collect and traffic drugs from big cities. We understand what debt bondage is now — and how it can be used to entrap you.

This conversation has moved on to what that risk is and what it involves.

This includes prosecution — and how prosecution for these offences can stop you from travelling internationally or from getting the type of job that you really want when you leave school. We've paid attention to how getting into crime has a way of stopping you from being able to get out of it again – and how few people want to give you another chance once you've made those mistakes (particularly after you turn 18).

We've had a really frank discussion about the risks involved in drug dependency – and the dangers that come along with abusing different types of drugs. I've been really honest and upfront with you about what you can expect from those drugs if you do use them – and why people enjoy using them to begin with, and why they are tempting. I've given you references to independent sources of advice so that you can test and verify what I've been saying for yourself (which I think is really important too).

The attraction to drugs and easy money through crime is something that can overwhelm your life quite easily and it can happen to anyone – so we've looked at that. We've also looked at what can be done if you've found yourself in that position. If you are in that position – sooner or later you will ask yourself *"How do I get my life back?"*. I hope that what I've written for you – which is my best and most honest advice – helps you to do that.

We can't be shy about this – if you've got into organised crime and County Lines – getting out of it is not easy and few people do get out of it undamaged. It damages people in lots and lots of ways. I'm being perfectly upfront about that. Getting out is about going through a painful barrier and it will test your courage. You'll have to trust me – and I really hope that you do – when I say that you *can* get your life back, and if you want it, you can be helped.

I hope that by using this book you have made a contract with yourself to get your life back – to identify the negativity in your life and to get away from it permanently. I hope you realise now that you have made mistakes that – sure, you're probably not proud of – but they are mistakes that lots of other people have also made, and they are lessons that you will learn from. Nobody is judging you – I just want you to turn a corner that goes towards a healthier and happier future.

With reading this book I do hope that I have underlined the value of talking to people – the people you trust, but also experts and professionals. That seeking help with anxiety and fear is a positive thing. That speaking to pastoral leaders in school is a good idea. Drug counselling is available and it is a supportive and positive thing too. Do not isolate yourself from people who genuinely love and care about you.

We've talked about seeking help – and who the best people are for you to go to – we considered the complications of talking to Mum or Dad. We have considered how we might use a professional to help us tell Mum or Dad about any trouble we might have got into. We thought about teachers, pastoral leaders, religious leaders, counsellors and friends. In giving thought to this we've also talked about why it's not a good idea to rely only on friends, or speaking to the people who supply drugs, about what you should do next.

We have considered the internet as a resource for support and advice – and how careful you have to be about trusted accredited sites and groups. I highlighted 'Talk to Frank' as an example of a good site that offers confidential personal advice and guidance to young people. As one of the additional pieces at the end of this book I will offer a list of reliable accredited online sources for advice about drugs, County Lines, criminal exploitation, sexual harm and exploitation.

We know how to be wary of unreliable sites and people online – and how we check those sources out to see if they are credible or whether they might be fake or fraudulent.

The important thing about seeking help is to build up your courage to reach out to good independent people who can help you to make objective decisions as opposed to 'subjective' decisions that are only made from your position alone. Allowing other people with expertise and knowledge to help you make decisions leads to better outcomes – but you have to be ready to sometimes take advice that you don't want to hear. Asking enough people so that you eventually find someone who will give you the advice you were hoping to get is a counter-productive exercise and the people who you went to originally will be unlikely to want to help you in future if they see that is what you have been doing. Try to surround yourself with a small number of reliable people that you can turn to for advice and guidance regularly. This makes it less likely that you will simply allow unhelpful people into your life at crucial moments.

Considering advice and guidance, we have talked about how we help our friends. This is a complicated subject. Your friend might be showing a number of signs and symptoms of being drawn into gang behaviour or selling illegal drugs – but they might not be receptive to your efforts that are intended to help them change.

Friends who do not want advice can become hostile towards you and we talked about trying to decide when to walk away from that situation – knowing that you cannot force someone to change.

When someone is worried or unhappy and they do want to change, we have talked about the best steps for you to take. Having confirmed or satisfied yourself that there is a problem – anticipating and being ready to answer certain important questions is important. Also being ready to understand that you are not supposed to solve this problem all on your own – and that going to ask for help from someone who is trained and experienced is not a sign of weakness, it's a wise thing to do.

We have talked about how instrumental your help is – being available to help a good friend on an emotional level. Helping a friend to make the right decision and to seek the type of help and support they need is incredibly important.

Within this, while we have discussed the need to support our friends, we have recognised two clear models of behaviour that people go through when they are dealing with drug dependency issues – the grief cycle being one (shock/denial, pain/guilt. Anger/bargaining, depression, the upward turn, reconstruction and eventually acceptance/hope). We considered how being rehabilitated from drug dependency can resemble grief and loss – and how getting out of being caught up in a drug, and a cycle of making money through crime can resemble over-coming a broken heart and an abusive relationship. We considered how going through this might involve going through depression too (which is a very real clinical illness).

Above all we have considered how seeking help can be an incredibly difficult thing. It can feel like 'snitching' and it might even make your friend very angry – but at the same time it might just prevent them from making the type of mistake that could change their lives forever, result in serious injury or loss, or even cost a life.

We appreciate that seeking help is a very difficult thing to do – and that having strong personal boundaries when a friend is refusing to accept help is very important. Also, when you do give help and support – it is so important to have the intelligence to know what the limits of your help and support are. You must never get isolated or cornered so that you carry the whole weight of the situation upon yourself alone.

The final thoughts that we have given in this book are to looking forward to a better future.

I think we understand now that people have come to this book, and the advice within it, from very different places. We all have things in our life that hold us back – and certainly some very much more than others. Having an appreciation for that

– I can tell that the inducements offered by people who want you to get involved in County Lines and drug dealing or criminal exploitation are a lot more tempting to some than others.

So we've tried to look for ways to put those offers into a certain context. Thinking about the short term nature of some of those things that people might ask you to trade your freedom and your future for.

We've thought about how we can be so driven and motivated by consumer products that we actually endanger and risk the rest of our lives – perhaps for a pair of trainers, perhaps for a mobile phone, possibly for less.

For people who feel trapped by the County Lines' system I have underlined the protection that is given through the Modern Day Slavery Act 2015 *– and the defence that any criminal actions they have felt compelled to do while being trafficked are not their criminal liability, but will be held against the people who trafficked them.*

I repeat this as a key piece of legislation which shows that 'the system' – the law – the police and the authorities are not out to arrest and convict children. The aim and the objective is to help young people to escape criminal exploitation.

Looking forward to better things is about making it a priority to know ourselves. Seeing through the fake or the false offers that are given by criminal gangs. Looking at the incentives of criminal gains – the electronics, the clothes and the trainers – to actually realise what you want your future to really be.

We've talked about changing the way we think, and in doing so adjusting the way that we see the world. How we sometimes fail to see the good in our lives because we are so preoccupied with the negative things instead.

We have spent time looking at how we can condition ourselves in a different way – to become more sympathetic, empathetic and compassionate people. How we can be more positive and optimistic. How we can become resilient to minor setbacks – coming to see them as lessons learned, instead of failures.

We have looked at the wonderful opportunity that we have to open our minds towards – the things we didn't know about. The jobs that we never knew existed – like becoming a marine biologist, or moving to a warm new country to start a new business.

We've considered the value of setting our own goals that are based on the things that we feel are important – not being compelled to do things by criminal organisations, or by people who stand by and criticise or undermine us.

I told you about how great people overcame their personal obstacles to make amazing contributions in the world. People like Roger Bannister, Amelia Earhart or Thomas Edison.

The world is full of incredible examples that we can learn from – and knowing that a particular job or role exists means that you can learn how you can qualify to do it, and how you can go about getting that position for yourself.

We also thought about how other people had the vision to imagine a role that they *wanted* – reshape a world around the way they thought it ought to be or was going to be. From people like Bill Gates or Steve Jobs, so others who in their own much smaller way used their personal passion and drive to create the life that they wanted to live (however unlikely it might have seemed at one time to everybody else).

I want to leave you – having talked about the risks around criminal exploitation – feeling much more positive about the things that you can do instead. About the real success that comes with investing time and effort in building a future that matters more to you, gives more to the world, and rewards you with things you really want.

There is no doubt whatsoever that at this moment in time – as I write this – we are living through very unsettling times. The Brexit transition is a change that worries a lot of people and will undoubtedly make a difference to the country as a whole. COVID-19 and the global health pandemic has completely changed the way that we conduct our lives – and many people are worried about how and when we can ever get back to 'normal'. We have all been touched by that – and some of us have experienced grief and bereavement because we have lost loved ones to the terrible coronavirus. We don't need very much more to make this world feel hostile and dangerous. The additional threat of criminal gangs targeting young people is incredibly unwelcome – now more than at any other time – but this is something that we've been (collectively) slow to respond to in an effective way.

The first and most important step is considering how young people can be equipped with a view towards self-defence – avoiding this nightmare, and helping each other to maintain safety in young communities.

Knowing about the threat – being able to identify it at a distance is certainly important. Knowing how to respond to it when it confronts you, or having knowledge that it is present in your community or it is targeting your friends or your friendship group is equally important.

The aim of this book has been to give you enough information to help you get to that point. To help you make good strong decisions. My perspective is, and always has been, that if young people are given the truth, plenty of information, and the time and space to think about it – the vast majority will make very positive decisions.

Those who make mistakes need help and support to get their lives back together – we shouldn't be angry at them, we shouldn't pity them. We need to demonstrate the values of sympathy, empathy and compassion. We need to help them recover and get back on their feet.

The anger of society should be reserved for criminal gangs who target and exploit young people at an increasingly young age.

When young people and the professionals, the subject matter experts, the people in counselling roles, people in law enforcement – work together, we create a very real opportunity to eradicate (that is completely wipe out), this terrible, awful form of crime.

Reading this book, you have a hugely important role to play. You can step forward to protect yourself, to protect your friends and to protect your community. By sharing your knowledge and your awareness of what is happening inside your year group, your peer group, or in your local part of town – you help everyone to shine a light into the murky hidden behaviour of organised criminal gangs.

I hope that this book has given you the confidence, the courage and the awareness that you need to do the right things when you see County Lines appearing in your local area. We do know that it is out there – sadly – and growing quickly. We do know that together we can stop it.

What follows in the 'appendices' of this book are some of the resources that I've referred to, but perhaps in a bit more detail.

This is going to include:

- A guide to the signs and symptoms of County Lines so that you can spot them easily;
- A quick guide on what to do when you do spot those signs of County Lines;

- A reference sheet of reliable online resources for people that you can speak to under different circumstances;

Please do look at and use these tools and guides. They are designed to help you and support you. I hope the way that I have put them together for you is something that works for you and is something that you can come back to from time to time if you need to.

APPENDIX 1 – The Signs and Symptoms

Signs and Symptoms:

You've got a friend, you've known them for a long time, but all of a sudden, they've changed:

- They have new fancy designer possessions and you can't really explain where they've come from (mobile phone, trainers, clothing…);
- They start changing their mobile phone frequently or you know that they are carrying more than one mobile phone;
- They've changed their friendship group and you're seeing less of them. They're getting distant and you don't know the people they are moving towards or the people they are moving towards are definitely into drink/drugs;
- They've become angry, hostile, confrontational and their moods seem irrational and difficult to explain;
- They're suddenly not coming into school regularly and they're missing lessons too;
- They've started going missing from home – maybe their mum and dad have asked

you if they know where they've been going?
- They're no longer interested in things that they used to be – abandon the football team, gymnastics, music or clubs and societies unexpectedly;
- They start talking about making trips into London or to another big city alone – maybe asking you to come along;
- You know that they've started experimenting with drugs and they're talking to you about it;
- They want you to start doing drugs or joining them in risk taking behaviours that you're uncomfortable with;
- They are selling drugs to friends or other people in or outside of school;
- You know they've started carrying a weapon habitually and they seem paranoid or have even threatened you;

It's far more likely that your friend will be open with you about their behaviour and a key issue will be that you may receive disclosures that they don't give to anyone else.

If they become more secretive – *for example you know that something is 'going on'* – but they won't be straight with you about it, that is also a concern.

If they start asking you to keep secrets for them — *but they won't tell you why* — that is worrying. We've talked about people getting you to cover for them when they stay away from home overnight. That is a key example.

Be very wary about keeping secrets or covering for people — particularly when they won't tell you *why*. If someone asks you to provide a false alibi — *that is they ask you to say that they were somewhere that you know they weren't* — this is a major red flag.

Friends *do* keep secrets for each other — but you should never give anyone an assurance that you will keep absolutely anything (no matter what it is) secret. There's a difference between not telling other people who they fancy, and helping them to store or sell drugs.

If a friend asks you to get involved in any behaviour — such as holding onto money for example — or hiding a package (and specifically if they won't tell you what is inside it) — you really need to question that behaviour. These are warning signs.

"Help me to hide this — it's my Mum's birthday present and I don't want her to find it"

"Oh lovely what is it?"

"Oh, er, it's er, a purse"

Two weeks later:

"Can you hide this? It's a present for my Dad…"

Additionally you know about your friend – probably better than anyone – if they start using a false accent, adopting a false voice, or using strange slang terms that you've never heard them use before, these are things that – in combination with the other points raise significant concerns.

If they start to develop an 'alter-ego' – a second personality, that dresses differently, talks different, and behaves very differently depending on who they are in front of – this can be a concern. We all behave slightly differently in different company – but we are talking about very obvious differences. Completely different dress sense, voice, accent and possibly they 'blank' or 'ghost' you or other people when they adopt this alter ego.

Appendix 2 – Responding to Signs & Symptoms

Here's a quick check list of how you might respond to the signs and symptoms that you've observed:

1. Have a private conversation with your friend. Emphasise that you've known them a long time and that you care about them. Consider how they respond are they:
   a. Receptive and asking for help?
   b. Worried and anxious?
   c. Angry and hostile?
   d. Offended – but struggling to explain?
2. Look for professional help. Talk to a trusted adult. Be discreet but don't keep your fears to yourself. Find a person you really respect and look up to, talk it through with them. Hand the situation over to a professional.

3. Decide early on whether you want to remain anonymous or not. Talk to your parents and other adults you trust about the pros and cons of going 'on the record' about your fears.
4. Keep yourself safe – *it is your first priority* – do not intervene in any situation physically that puts you in risk of harm. Allow professional agencies to protect your friend.
5. Be aware that you may have to walk away from your friend for a period of time to protect yourself. You can only offer them help – you can't make them accept your help.
6. If and when your friend starts to resurface from their ordeal, be ready to forgive them for their mistakes. Use sympathy, empathy and compassion to help them to get their life back together.
7. Try not to blame them for making the mistakes that they have made. As much as you can – avoid being another voice in their life that judges them and tells them that they are a bad person. It is only more likely to drive them into alienation.
8. Don't make public knowledge of a private crisis. Once you have handed the matter to the adults and professionals that you

trust, don't make it a subject of conversation for anyone who might be interested. Always keep it off the internet and social media.

9. Be kind to yourself. Even if you can't prevent your friend from coming to serious harm – you are doing your best, you have done your best, you can do no more. *This is not your fault*.

10. Do not allow yourself to be drawn into whatever is going on. Keep your distance. Maintain your focus on the things that you want to achieve. Stay positive and stay safe.

If the situation that you have observed or gained knowledge of has caused you anxiety or fear you have a right to ask for help and support. Reach out to your school and ask them to get you some assistance to work through any emotional or mental health anxieties that you have recognised in yourself. Never be afraid to ask for the support that you need.

Appendix 3 – Support Services and Resources:

https://www.talktofrank.com/

This is an independent website that offers free advice and guidance about all manner of drugs and psychoactive substances. They offer free and anonymous drug counselling without an appointment between 2PM and 6PM every day. You can also call this service on 0300 1236600.

https://www.nspcc.org.uk/

The National Society for the Prevention Cruelty to Children is the leading child protection charity in the UK. They offer a range of resources to support parents, children and professionals – including sound advice and guidance on how to spot abuse. They also have a helpline – 0808 800 5000 and trained counsellors are available to offer help, advice and support. The NSPCC also support parents who are struggling with drug and alcohol issues of their own.

https://www.childrenssociety.org.uk/what-is-county-lines

The Children's* Society is another exceptional charity which promotes the health and wellbeing of children and young people. They have excellent resources explaining the threat of County Lines, what it is, who it affects, and what to do if you identify a child involved in criminal exploitation.

https://www.childline.org.uk

Any child or young person can call Childline for free on 0800 1111 (yes that's the whole number – not a typo). As well as helping young people with information about the threat of crime, Childline can help with coping mechanisms to support depression, anxiety, loneliness and feelings of isolation. Childline is very much about supporting children who have suffered early life trauma and adverse childhood experiences – they have a section for children with parents in prison, drugs and other matters. They have a 1-2-1 secure chatroom for counselling. They have some great resources.

https://www.nationalcrimeagency.gov.uk/

The National Crime Agency website is a really informative resource. This also contains links to the Child Exploitation and Online Protection Command (CEOP) and links that allow you to contribute information/intelligence. You can follow the Director General of the NCA on twitter – she tweets regularly - @NCA_LynneOwens – and this is definitely an account that I would recommend anyone to follow.

https://crimestoppers-uk.org/

You can call CrimeStoppers at any time on 0800 555 111 with regard to information about any form of criminality in any part of the United Kingdom. This is a brilliant charity and they pass information through to local police forces promptly and effectively. You don't have to give your name and you won't be traced on the basis of what you provide. For many people this is reassurance enough for them to give information that makes a critical difference to drugs enforcement in their local area.

https://www.fearless.org/en

Is a source of information for children and young people about crime and criminality. Young people can supply information with 100% confidentiality. They have a very up front but contemporary style in their presentation and they also link to other great resources (including some of the ones I have cited here). They have information on County Lines and the Criminal Exploitation of Children specifically.

https://www.mind.org.uk/

Mind are a tremendous charity that support the vital agenda of improving mental health for everyone. They have fantastic resources that reach across into the issue of drugs and psychoactive substance misuse and dependency. They have a section dedicated to children and young people which is invaluable.

http://www.marijuana-anonymous.org.uk/

Cannabis dependency is a real issue – a genuine problem – for adults and young people. MA have great resources to help you to identify whether your use of the drug has become a problem that you are struggling to get out of. They provide a pressure free environment, a non-judgemental context, and a host of information that is vital for anyone who needs to turn the corner on Cannabis dependency. You can call them on 0300 124 0373.

https://www.relate.org.uk/

Relationship crisis – whether it is between parents, or parent and child directly, can be a source of emotional distress that makes it impossible for a child to seek the advice and guidance that they need. Relate are possibly the best known service for helping people to mediate their problems and sort things out.

https://www.cruse.org.uk/

In the worst case scenario you might suffer bereavement, and that can be the very worst type of emotional distress that you ever have to deal with. Unfortunately in life we will always have to deal with death and loss. Cruse are the largest and best known charity that offers support to people in all types of circumstances struggling with loss of a loved one. You can call them on 0808 808 1677.

SUBVERSIVEMEDIA
PUBLICATIONS

Copyright © 2020 Philip Priestley

All rights reserved. No part of this publication may be reproduced, distributed or transmitted in any form or by any means, including photocopying, recording or other electronic or mechanical methods without the prior written permission of the publisher, except in the case of brief quotations embodied in critical reviews and certain other non-commercial uses permitted by copyright law. For permission requests please email the publisher addressed "Attention: Permissions Coordinator" at the following address:

SMP@inclusive-development.co.uk

Publisher's Cataloguing-in-Publication data:
Priestley, Philip
County Lines: A Young Person's Guide / Phil Priestley

ISBN: 978-1-8382131-0-7

1. Main category of the book – Non-fiction
2. Other category – Child protection
3. Sociology
4. Self Help

FIRST EDITION

www.ingramcontent.com/pod-product-compliance
Lightning Source LLC
Chambersburg PA
CBHW071731080526
44588CB00013B/1979